FULL FRONTAL

Of related interest from Faber and Faber

SEX, LIES AND VIDEOTAPE
by Steven Soderbergh

GETTING AWAY WITH IT
Or: The Further Adventures of the
Luckiest Bastard You Ever Saw
Starring Steven Soderbergh
Also starring Richard Lester as
The Man Who Knew More Than He Was Asked

TRAFFIC
by Stephen Gaghan
introduction by Steven Soderbergh and Stephen Gaghan

FULL FRONTAL

Coleman Hough

faber and faber

First published in 2002
by Faber and Faber Limited
3 Queen Square London WC1N 3AU
Published in the United States by Faber and Faber Inc.
an affiliate of Farrar, Straus and Giroux LLC, New York

Typeset by Country Setting, Kingsdown, Kent CT14 8ES
Printed in England by Mackays of Chatham plc, Chatham, Kent

A CIP record for this book
is available from the British Library

ISBN 0–571–21643–9

2 4 6 8 10 9 7 5 3 1

CONTENTS

'DO IT YOURSELF' FILMMAKING

AN INTERVIEW WITH STEVEN SODERBERGH BY ROB NUELL

What inspired you to do this movie?

It just grew out of a desire to turn to a more small-scale project. The movies were getting progressively bigger, peaking with *Ocean's Eleven*. So while I was preparing *Ocean's Eleven*, I was hatching the idea to go and do something small, and Coleman Hough and I had been talking about script ideas, using some one-acts that she had written as a jumping-off point. I decided on a time frame that we would follow no matter what, and it worked out that way. I've been very lucky in that regard.

So was this an attempt, in a way, to get back to your roots?

No, it was just that I don't like to follow one experience with a similar experience. I've been happy with the progression of the last few movies: *The Limey* was very different from *Erin*, which was very different from *Traffic*, which was very different from *Ocean's*, and *Full Frontal* again was a way to try a different aesthetic. I try and create a new aesthetic for each film, that's what's fun to me. Some directors have an aesthetic that they use on every film and they look for material that will fit what they do, I work the opposite way. *Traffic* is a run-and-gun movie on a literal level, but *Full Frontal* was run-and-gun on a conceptual level. At the time I made *Schizopolis*, this whole DV wave was just starting, and the technology available wasn't as elegant as it is now. We shot that in 1995, so it turned out that the cheap way to do it was to buy some old film gear for very little money, and shoot on 35 mm. We shot off and on for ten months with a five-person crew. That was the way to do it then, this is the way to do it now, or seems to be, although obviously we're still shooting some film that's integrated with the video, but for a very specific reason. And I'm enjoying it.

Although this isn't technically a sequel, you call this your follow-up to sex, lies, and videotape.

We're calling it the 'unauthorized sequel' to *sex, lies, and videotape*.

And what are some of the similarities?

Well, it's a character-based film about a group of people dancing off each other and colliding. If somebody came to me and said, 'I want you do to a version of *sex, lies, and videotape* today,' this is what I would come up with. It's a cousin to that, or at least that's how I sold it to Harvey.

You sent out a list of rules attached to the script. All of these seemed to be necessary requests to stay within the film's scope and budget. Was there trepidation on the part of the actors?

Well, the last rule was if you're not happy about the previous rules you can just stop reading and send the script back. So everybody went forward. I assumed that to enter into a contract with us meant they wanted to play along, and they all did. The point was to give them as much responsibility as they could handle for their characters. That's my approach. I don't bother the actors a lot. Only when they are having a problem do I get in their way. I wanted to take that idea of giving them responsibility to the furthest extreme that I could, even to the point of doing these interviews while we were shooting with them. They had to improvise in character at length about what they were going through, so in a sense they were writing for us. And, I'm still in the process of figuring out how to incorporate that material because I'm only using the audio. But it was a really helpful tool for us, it was an experiment that made me think of their characters in a different way, and it made them think about their characters in a different way, and it was something that I may actually do on other films knowing that I won't use it, but just as an exercise. It was pretty fascinating to watch them fuse themselves with a fictional character in front of you, because I knew them well enough to sense when they were borrowing from their life and when they were just making it up.

And did any of the script change based on this footage?

A little bit. One thing that came up (which should have been really evident before) was on the first or second day of shooting, somebody said the way Catherine Keener and Mary McCormack's characters relate is almost like sisters. Coleman and I had never talked about it, but as soon as I heard it I thought, well, yeah, of course they should be sisters. So we changed it. It may have even been Catherine who said, 'Gee, it feels like I'm talking to one of my sisters.'

And did their relationship get more interesting?

Yeah, I think so, because then this whole thing developed about their shared past and events that had happened in their past that they've both experienced but had very different reactions to. That all happened kind of early, those discussions, and it really did colour the way they behaved toward each other, and that was really helpful. But within this free-style way of working we had a very rigid schedule, and I do believe in parameters, I do think you need to have laws, and walls, to make you think laterally instead of vertically all the time. And so we worked quickly, and the days that we shot on DV, the actors said they would go home exhausted because all day, the entire day, they were acting.

And how closely did they stick to what was written in the script?

Pretty close. Within actual scenes there wasn't a lot of improvisation. Mostly editing. We would say, oh, the scene's too long, or there's an emotional transition that's a little tricky, maybe we should reorder things. I remember a couple times with Catherine and Mary, in some of their longer dialogue scenes, at lunch we edited and restructured some of their conversation. But all of the lines that remain were in the script. I think you do need to feel like you have time to edit and weigh things, so the great thing about shooting on DV is that you can stop for an hour, if you need to, and really work the scene to get it to where you want. And as soon as you get it to where you want it, five minutes later you're shooting it. And so that was a great luxury, and I think it results in performances that are extremely immediate.

How did the spy cam work?

The spy cam came out because I was talking to Paul Ledford (Sound Mixer) one day, and he said, 'I need a way to see the set so I can talk to my boom operator.' So he got this little lipstick cam, and we would work at finding a place in each set-up, because I'm shooting the scenes in their entirety from beginning to end, and I would come back every once in a while to the sound cart and I would see the angles that Paul had gotten, and they were invariably kind of interesting in a weird way. So I said, 'Let's start recording this. Start recording it when the camera cuts, and then stop recording it when the camera starts. Keep the mics up and just see what happens.' So we ended up with six, seven hours of footage, a lot of it which can never see the light of day. And there isn't much of it in the movie, but there is some of it. Again, it was just an experiment.

Was everyone aware that they were being filmed by the spy cam?

No. But having done it, I'll definitely do it again at some point. I have ideas about how to make it work, how to use it in a way that you can really integrate it into the movie organically.

Sort of like a Day for Night *type situation.*

Yeah, yeah. There's definitely something there. But again, it was part of the experiment.

⋆

What do you think DV has changed about the industry?

I think its impact potentially goes beyond just people working in that format. I think it makes people who don't work in that format reconsider what they're doing a little bit. I mean, a lot of people are thinking about it, even the people that aren't working in this way, and I think for audiences there's less patience with what I call a movie that is directed from the back of a limousine. I think people want to feel like things are happening in front of them.

The immediacy of the medium.

Yeah. But at the end of the day, it's still going to come down to filmmakers with an interesting story using that medium.

It seems to put the emphasis back on storytelling.

Well, but here's the problem. It's really easy to just go out and shoot something, but it's not right for everything. You do need to consider carefully whether this is the right aesthetic for the story you're trying to tell, or whether it's distracting. It's not a panacea for what's ailing the film industry.

DV seems to have been really embraced in Europe, especially Denmark. Do you think it just comes down to the fact that it lets filmmakers make films on their own terms that are also commercially viable?

No, I think it's just a reaction to the fact they can't compete on a mainstream filmmaking level because they don't have the resources that we have available over here. So again, they're thinking laterally: 'What do we have? Well, we have interesting ideas. And maybe we'll go in the opposite direction, the complete opposite direction,' which I think is a great idea. It's the same thing that happened in music in the early eighties when people got tired of corporate rock. Technology was getting a little better, and people could record shit in their garages or on the cheap that sounded pretty cool. And I feel like that's happening here. The question is how to reach the audiences the way they were able to, and you know the web can be part of that.

Yeah.

I was just reading that one of the guys that formed Slamdance, they're gonna put DVDs of his movie in *Total Film and Video* magazine, so it's going to be like 350,000 copies. And I wouldn't mind doing that. If I said, 'All right, I'm gonna do something, I don't know what the hell it is, I'm going to shoot it in three weeks, and it'll be ninety minutes long, and it'll cost twenty-five grand, and let's put it out in the magazine. That's how we're gonna release it.' And that got me excited, like, wow, you can just go out and sketch . . . I like the idea of somebody buying it on a newsstand and taking it home and putting it on their television. I'm intrigued by that. I don't have a 'well, unless my movie plays in a theatre it's not a movie' attitude. I'm interested in what I consider to be kind of bootleg operations.

Have you discussed this with other directors?

Oh, absolutely, absolutely. Like I said, it's on everybody's mind. I have director friends who've never worked in this way who bombard me with questions about working this way. I think they're trying to determine whether or not it's something they would want to do. They're very intrigued by it.

But maybe a little unsure about whether to take the plunge . . .

Well, there's a quote that those who are used to working with the least can invariably work with the most, but those who are used to working with the most have real difficulty working with the least. And I think that's true. I came up through the sort of 'do it yourself' indie world, and I think one of the reasons I've been able to be cavalier about my choices for regular movies is that in the back of my mind I know I can always go and raise a few hundred thousand dollars to make something on the cheap. I always have that, and I'll always go back to that. So I always felt like, well, if the town ends up totally rejecting me – and I went through a period where nobody was really interested in seeing what I was up to – I can go back. I went back and started over and made *Schizopolis*, and *Gray's Anatomy* as a way of creatively getting excited again.

Do you think everything will be shot digitally, say, fifteen years from now?

No. I think we'll be shooting film for a long time. It's a tool, and it's beautiful, and it does things photochemically that you'll never be able entirely to recreate. So as a capture medium I think it's always going to be there. What's going to change is the projection. I'm a huge proponent of digital projection. *Ocean's* was the widest digital cinema release so far, and it was really at our insistence because I love it, and I can't wait until that's the norm. It solves so many problems, including the fact that the industry spent seven hundred million dollars in prints last year. They just get thrown into the trash at the end of the day.

What directors did you see embracing this early on?

You know, Godard was light years ahead of the curve. He's been working in this way for two decades now. He saw it way before anybody else did. And I've watched a lot of the films that he's made on video, and they're really fascinating. But he's unique, he's open to everything. He's a real artist, and is totally unconcerned with anything but keeping himself excited and engaged. And that's why he is who he is. I think if you're a certain kind of director it's difficult to move into working this way without having to answer questions like, 'So are you slumming conceptually? Is that what you're doing? You live in this big house, and you're going to come down to the poor section of town and drive around for a couple weeks and then go back home?' I think that's an issue for a lot of directors.

It's almost like a lifestyle decision for some people.

Yeah, I guess it is, and I guess it really comes down to what's important to you. *It is* a personality thing, *it is* a character thing. And *I really like the sensation* - even on *Ocean's* - of making the film with my own hands. That's why I've been working toward this idea of shooting everything myself. I was trying to make a big movie that still felt hand-tooled. That's what gets me up in the morning, that sensation. That was the challenge of *Ocean's*: can I keep that level of proximity to a movie made on that scale? It was really just a test, and I came out the other side of it thinking, yes, you can, but it's more fun when it's two million bucks and not ninety.

*

How many people were on the crew for Full Frontal*?*

On DV days, eight or nine, maybe ten at the most. On the film days, maybe fifteen. Really small.

And the film was shot over four weeks?

Eighteen days. And actually we re-shot a day and a half of material within the eighteen days because I realised that I'd made all these rules for the actors but I hadn't really made a set of rules for myself. And midway through the second day I realised that I needed to do that, and when I started thinking about what those rules would be I realised that the first day-and-a-half I hadn't conformed to them. And so on the third day we started re-shooting the first day-and-a-half, and eventually we caught up.

What about the equipment you used? How did you end up choosing the equipment? I think you used cameras from Canon?

Well, we did our research and we were looking for hardware and software that was powerful and yet flexible. I checked out a lot of different cameras and I just really liked the Canon XL-1, and the XL-1S had even more things on it that I could take advantage of. My whole idea was, it has to look like it was shot by an amateur. So I literally used it the way it came out of the box. I used their lens,

I didn't put any extra gear on it, I held it the way Joe Shmo would. That was my whole thing: I have to shoot it like anybody else. And, I was really happy. The camera turned out to be incredibly robust, and flexible, it really influenced the way I would stage and shoot scenes because I could do almost anything I could think of. So there's a lot of movement. This one shot – I don't know if it'll survive the movie – I had the lipstick cam on the roof of a car as it approached a hotel and then followed the passenger out of the car into the lobby. On film that would have taken three days, *if*, if you could have done it at all. It would have been a rigging nightmare. And this was the sort of flexibility you had, I mean it was like playing.

You were like a kid with a camera?

Yeah. The camera was really ideal for us. And then Final Cut Pro is also a very powerful system, and ideally suited to a project like this, and we've taken advantage of what it can do in terms of playing around with imagery, and being lean and mean, trying to do things efficiently.

What filmmaking tool would you like to invent?

You know what I'd like to invent? Two things. And this actually came out of using the Canon. There were all these read-outs in the frame - what my exposure was, what my shutter speed was, all this information and I really liked that. It made me think I'd love to have that in a film camera. And there's no reason, to me, that you shouldn't be able to have a lens that generates a read-out of your focus setting that you can see, and that the assistant can see. You know the actor's at eleven-feet-six, and they've missed their mark by half a foot, and you have to go six inches. So, I'd love to have a read-out in the lenses of film cameras. Some people might find it distracting, but I found it comforting to know I'm at the f-stop that I want, and what the shutter speed is, and the white balance setting . . .

Especially when you're working quickly.

Yeah. And the other is – I'm a very big believer in keeping the audience comfortable and oriented, and one of the things that makes them comfortable and oriented is when all the eye-lines are correct. So I'm a stickler about the angle of somebody's eye-line – not just that they're looking left, but they're looking four-and-a-half-feet left at the lens which means when we turn around we need to make sure the other person's looking four-and-a-half-feet the other way. So I want to invent something that just calculates that third side of the triangle. You could probably just use a tape measure. Anyway, just stupid shit like that.

So how does the internet tie into this project?

Well, we didn't have time to realise it on this film, but what I would like to do someday on a project like this is to have the spy cam go into the website all day, so you can just log on and see what's happening on the set. I'm sure there are huge legal ramifications to this. But again, if you designed it, put it on the cover page, made it one of the rules that the video tap and/or the spy cam will be going to the website all day, maybe you could do it. I think it would be fun for people to watch what the process is, how a shot gets made – like, okay, they're moving locations but keep the thing running – 'We're packin' up, we're movin'' . . . that's something that I think would be really fun to do.

So the Full Frontal *website is a step in that direction?*

Yeah, but on the next one, two weeks before we start shooting we need to hand everyone a username and passcode and let them know, this is how you enter a diary, and it'll be posted the minute you submit it. I think that would be a blast. Then we could all stop doing junkets.

So do you have a favourite digital film?

Julien Donkey-Boy. I just loved everything about it. I liked the way they really took advantage of what you can do in that format, in terms of how scenes are staged and the content of the scenes. And I loved what they did with the footage, how they manipulated it. I thought it was pretty spectacular-looking. But more than anything it was a movie where they got better stuff for having shot that way, because there was this level of intimacy, and spontaneity, that clearly was a result of being able to shoot anything anywhere. I just thought it really worked, and that it wasn't accidental. It was very well thought out.

And well crafted.

And that's the problem with the DV aesthetic, the trick of combining the enthusiasm of the amateur with the rigorous approach of the professional – trying to keep those two things together. And that's what I thought *Julien* had. The energy of someone for whom this isn't a job. He's an artist, and he takes his work seriously enough to know again there are parameters and there is a structure.

So that was an influence on how you approached making Full Frontal*?*

Yeah, *Julien* was a big influence. I think Harmony [Korine] is insanely talented. I think he's made two really fascinating films, and I don't know why more people aren't talking about them. When I saw *Gummo,* having read very little positive stuff about it, I thought it was great. If somebody said to me, 'I want you to show me what most of middle America is like,' I'd go, 'Well, you should watch *Gummo,*' because that's been my experience of growing up in mid-sized towns, mostly in the South. There's houses where people never throw anything away. I've been in houses like that. The desultory nature of most people's lives and this inarticulate anger that's below the surface of everything. The threat of violence that is in the air because of their frustration – I thought it was palpable, and it didn't make me feel comfortable, although it sure felt familiar. And I don't know who else is doing that. I don't know who wants to. But I was still stunned after I saw the film that I hadn't read more serious film criticism saying that you need to pay attention to this.

Most critics I've read don't seem to know what to make of his films.

Yeah . . . like it's a gimmick, like he's just a kid. And *Julien* I thought was even better, more focused, more analytical, and so I think the guy's made a pair of really remarkable movies, and nobody seems to really give a shit. It's weird.

Can you talk a little bit about Richard Lester, and his influence on you?

What I like about Richard Lester, what I thought was infectious about his films - even the serious ones - was for all their style I still felt their priorities were telling a story. That and his range. He had a very eclectic list of films. I can't imagine two films more different than *A Hard Day's Night* and *Petulia*. I mean, completely different.

Different universes. And yet both of them masterpieces I think. And so part of my wanting to do that book, *Getting Away With It*, was talking to Lester to find out how that came to be, such an eclectic filmmaker when it came to material. Every time I turn people onto *Petulia* they call me back and say, 'Holy shit.'

His influence on filmmakers doesn't seem as apparent.

Well, I think it's sort of unspoken. But you know, you're always standing on the shoulders of somebody who came before you, and when I sat down and was trying to re-invigorate myself, when I thought of whose work I've admired and respected, and who I really wanted to talk to, it was him. He never made movies about himself, and that was a really important thing to recognize. I think the biggest difference between *Full Frontal* and *sex, lies, and videotape* is that it looks outward more than *sex, lies* did, even as I'm trying to burrow deeper into the characters than I did in *sex, lies*. There are things in it that I relate to, but it's not a movie about me, really. I didn't want it to be about me. *Full Frontal* is less overtly personal in that regard, and I think the perception of what constitutes a personal film is really skewed. I think people who write about movies don't quite understand what 'personal' means, and I think there's too much importance placed on it, this idea that if it's personal then it's more legitimate than something that is less personal. As someone who makes movies, I completely disagree. You know, I've been invested equally in everything I've done, whether it had something to do with me or not. I was as engaged and interested in *Ocean's Eleven* as I was in *sex, lies, and videotape* or *King of the Hill.* I have since gotten a lot of that 'personal' stuff out of my system. Part of it I think is just being young, in my twenties. I think the films have gotten better since I stopped navel-gazing. I know they're more fun to sit through.

THE RULES

IMPORTANT

If you are an actor considering a role in this film, please note the following:

1 All sets are practical locations.

2 You will drive yourself to the set. If you are unable to drive yourself to the set, a driver will pick you up, but you will probably become the subject of ridicule. Either way, you must arrive alone.

3 There will be no craft service, so you should arrive on set 'having had'. Meals will vary in quality.

4 You will pick, provide and maintain your own wardrobe.

5 You will create and maintain your own hair and make-up.

6 There will be no trailers. The company will attempt to provide holding areas near a given location, but don't count on it. If you need to be alone a lot, you're pretty much screwed.

7 Improvisation will be encouraged.

8 You will be interviewed about your character. This material may end up in the finished film.

9 You will be interviewed about the other characters. This material may end up in the finished film.

10 You will have fun whether you want to or not.

If any of these guidelines are problematic for you, stop reading now and send this screenplay back where it came from.

CAST AND CREW

MAIN CAST

NICHOLAS / CALVIN	Blair Underwood
CATHERINE / FRANCES	Julia Roberts
CARL	David Hyde Pierce
ALICE	Catherine Keener
LINDA	Mary McCormack
LUCY	Erika Alexander
MAVIS	Justina Machado
BRIAN	Rainn Wilson
JERRY	Jerry Weintraub
BILL / GUS	David Duchovny
ARTY / ED	Enrico Colantoni
HITLER	Nicky Katt

MAIN CREW

Directed by	Steven Soderbergh
Written by	Coleman Hough
Producer	Scott Kramer
Producer & First Assistant Director	Gregory Jacobs
Executive Producers	Harvey Weinstein & Bob Weinstein
Cinematography by	Steven Soderbergh
Film editing by	Sarah Flack

Full Frontal

EXT. NEW YORK. DAWN. TODAY.

The sleeping spires of the great city.

Cut.

INT. APARTMENT. DAWN.

Nicholas, black, late thirties, is sitting on the edge of a bed, looking down at a woman, naked, on the unmade bed. She's a white woman and she is asleep. His hand is on her back.

Cut.

EXT. TOWN CAR. DAWN.

Nicholas looks out the window as he is driven through the slowly brightening streets and highways to La Guardia Airport.

Cut.

INT. AIRPORT. DAY.

Nicholas sits near his departure gate, reading Los Angeles Magazine. *Brad Pitt is on the cover with his head shaved, trumpeting this edition as the 'Hair' issue. There is a small carry-on bag by his feet.*

A white woman, Catherine, approaches and sits down with some amount of purpose. She is smart and sexy.

Nicholas looks at her, thinking a moment before he says:

NICHOLAS

Catherine.

CATHERINE

Nicholas.

Cut.

Catherine and Nicholas seated in the first class departure lounge. There is a tape recorder in Catherine's hand. As they speak, someone checks their photo IDs.

NICHOLAS

– I play the partner.

CATHERINE

An equal partner?

NICHOLAS

(*smiles*)

All right, I'm his flunky, OK? Is that what you want to hear?

CATHERINE

Is that what you want me to write?

NICHOLAS

No. 'Sidekick' is fine. Really, though, I'm from TV, he's an established star. I have no problem with that. I don't expect to make the leap without working for it.

CATHERINE

Do you think any black actors get to make the leap without working for it? I mean, that seems to happen more often to white actors.

He looks at her.

NICHOLAS

Jesus, is this the kind of story you want to write? Because we can go there, I've got plenty of opinions.

CATHERINE

You want it to be boring.

NICHOLAS

Shit, let's go. I'm game.

Cut.

INT. PLANE. DAY.

First class. Nicholas and Catherine are seated next to each other.

NICHOLAS

Having a teacher that reaches you, that's what makes a difference. I remember I was in high school and I was going through a real asshole phase, fucking up a lot. And the drama teacher, who I liked, asked me what was going on. I sort of mumbled about not liking school, and she said, 'You're bored. You're bored because you're an artist, potentially, and artists only recognise the authority of other artists. But why are you taking that out on us?'

Catherine's tape recorder stops, as if on cue. She turns the tape over.

NICHOLAS

You transcribe those yourself?

She looks at him like, 'Are you fucking insane?' He makes a face like, 'How the hell should I know what you do with these things?'

CATHERINE

Someone at work.

NICHOLAS

Like an intern.

CATHERINE

Yeah.

She's got the new tape in now.

NICHOLAS

Male or female?

CATHERINE

What do you think?

NICHOLAS

Male. Which is it? And don't say you won't tell me.

CATHERINE

Give me a break. He's a guy. Do you want to know if he's straight?

NICHOLAS

Oh, I know he's straight.

She looks at him.

Cut.

EXT. LOS ANGELES. DAY.

Outlines emerging against a dirty suede sunrise.

Cut.

INT. HOUSE. DAWN.

A man, Carl, in bed beside his wife, Lee. He's a little past forty, balding, and awake. Lee is the same approximate age but asleep. She stirs suddenly and awakens. He closes his eyes.

LEE

Jesus.

She rises, takes a beat to orient herself and heads for the bathroom.

Cut.

Lee is in the shower. Carl is still in bed, his eyes open.

Cut.

Lee, crossing the room, half-dressed. Carl sits up in bed as though waking.

Cut.

Lee is completely dressed and preparing to exit the bedroom.

Cut.

Lee, at the kitchen table, finishing a handwritten note. Upon completion she places it in an envelope, writes 'Carl' on the front, and sets it on the kitchen counter.

Cut.

Carl, alone in the bedroom, putting on his tennis shoes.

Cut.

INT. KITCHEN. DAY.

Lee at the table, a dog at her feet. Carl enters, goes to the fridge.

LEE

(from the newspaper)

Another robbery at a pornographic bookstore. Fifth in two weeks.

CARL

Jesus.

LEE

They say the suspect is female.

CARL

Huh.

Beat.

So I had this dream, last night. In the dream, my job is to go to work every day and narrate a documentary about some guy's life. This is all I do every day, narrate eight hours of this guy's life from the previous day. Whether this is airing on television or something, I don't know. And he's like me, his life is like mine, and I'm realising I might learn something from this guy's life that I might apply to my own.

Lee puts the paper down and looks at Carl.

CARL

The problem is, I have no life to apply it to, because all I do every day is narrate this guy's life, go home, have dinner, go to bed, and go in to work the next day. I have no effect on anyone; I am just a voice that tells people about this guy's life.

Beat. Lee just stares at him.

CARL

Oh, and I pee green. In the dream I go to the bathroom and my urine is bright green.

Another beat as Lee stares at him.

LEE

Would you like my interpretation?

CARL

No.

Beat.

What's on for today?

LEE

More bloodshed.

CARL

God. How do you stand it?

LEE

(*thinking*)

There are days when I just want to lash out at them. They didn't *do* anything, and I'm feeling like . . .

Carl looks at her. She shifts gears.

LEE

Don't forget to make the brownies for Gus's party.

She leaves. Carl looks at the dog.

Cut.

INT. KITCHEN. DAY.

Carl gets ready to go, takes the brownies out and leaves them on the stove to cool. His cell phone rings. He can't find it.

Cut.

EXT. HOUSE. DAY.

Tableau of a middle-income dwelling. Carl heads for his car. Before reaching it, he looks across to see his neighbour, dressed as a vampire, picking up his morning newspaper.

Cut.

EXT. HOUSE. DAWN.

Tableau of a lower-income apartment duplex. Linda, thirty-five, locks her door, checks it three times, walks down the stairs – walks back up – checks it again. Across the street, her neighbour, a rock musician guy accompanied by a rock musician gal stroll to the curb and get on a motorcycle. Linda unlocks her door and goes back into her apartment.

INT. LINDA'S APT. DAWN.

Linda looks out the window at the motorcycle couple from a gap in her blinds.

We hear the motorcycle drive off. Linda walks towards her door.

Cut.

EXT. CAR. DAY.

Carl, in his car, staring ahead.

His car stops at a red light. Moments later, a car pulls up alongside Carl's. It is being driven by Linda. She waves. He waves back. The light seems long. They silently exchange friendly unvoiced greetings.

Linda is taking a left, so when Carl takes off in response to the green light, she slowly pulls into the intersection to wait for a break in oncoming traffic. We let Carl go and stay with her. And stay with her, as she waits, and waits. The car behind her honks, wanting her to move further forward.

LINDA

Oh, fuck you, you fu –

Cut.

EXT. CAR. DAY.

Later. Linda drives along, singing to her radio.

Cut.

INT. HOTEL ROOM. DAY.

Linda massaging a woman.

WOMAN

. . . and I wasn't saying yes, but I wasn't saying no either, and before I knew it I realised I was no longer in control of the situation. It wasn't violent, I just remember feeling I really wasn't OK with it, but I wasn't saying that out loud, I was saying it to myself. And then it was over. And I made sure I never, ever saw him again. I was nineteen.

A beat. Linda, digesting this:

LINDA

Could I turn you over now?

Cut.

INT. PLANE. DAY.

Nicholas and Catherine, single-serving breakfast in front of them, albeit first-class variety.

CATHERINE

You ever been to therapy?

NICHOLAS

No. That whole thing, I don't get it. It's like, they're just selling you back to yourself.

Cut.

Nicholas, in mid-sentence.

NICHOLAS

He owned these stores, called Superettes. They were bigger than a convenience store, but not as big as an actual supermarket. So he has these Superettes and me and my two brothers, we work in the Superettes from the time we're like fourteen or fifteen. Long-ass hours, really hard work. I mean, the profit margin is a joke. Eleven cents on a dollar fifty can of soup, right? Day in, day out. So then one day me and my brothers go to him and we say look, let's sell the Superettes and get into sporting goods, open a sporting goods store. Because we were all athletes and felt like it was something we could really do, you know? And we had it all figured out about this sports store, and we made this proposal to him, about selling the Superettes so we could start one. And he says, you don't know anything about sporting goods, nobody's gonna give you the money to do that, blah blah, just shutting us down. So we just quit, me and my brothers – we just quit, we quit working for him, and six months later all the Superettes went under. He never forgave us. I don't think we ever forgave him, either. We worked hard at those Superettes, I think we felt that . . . it felt like if we were together, me and my brothers, we could do anything.

Beat.

I sort of got over it, but my little brother . . . he was really mad that my dad didn't believe in us. He moved to Florida, my brother. The other one is in San Diego, and I'm here.

CATHERINE

He was how old when he died?

NICHOLAS

Sixty-three.

Nicholas takes a healthy bite of his meal.

NICHOLAS

I've made more in a month than my father made the last ten years of his life. That changes shit. People assume you're different. You become different in reaction to their new behaviour. They say you've changed. And back and forth.

CATHERINE

Well, have you?

NICHOLAS

What, changed? No and yes.

CATHERINE

How yes?

NICHOLAS

Let's just say, I feel relieved to have it because I never had it before. You look like you've always had it.

CATHERINE

Do I?

NICHOLAS

Have you?

CATHERINE

Always had it? You mean like from the beginning?

NICHOLAS

You know what I mean.

CATHERINE

I think I know what you mean, yes.

Nicholas takes another bite of his breakfast.

Cut.

INT. GARAGE. DAY.

Lee pulls into her space. She notices an inflated beach ball resting near her car.

Cut.

INT. OFFICE. DAY.

Lee walks down the hall to her office with the beach ball under her arm.

INT. CARL'S OFFICE. DAY.

The company logo is dominant in the hallway outside Carl's office. It says LA Magazine. *There is a large picture of Brad Pitt, running his hands through his hair on the current cover.*

Carl is talking to a female colleague (black), Lucy. They appear to be extremely good friends, but be aware of this: he is in love with her and she doesn't know it.

CARL

What's interesting is you can be paid to have sex by a company, to act in an adult film, but if some guy wants to pay you five hundred bucks to have sex, that's illegal.

LUCY

Right.

CARL

Porn is interesting, because I would imagine there are two reasons you're appearing in porn: you need money, or you're an exhibitionist.

LUCY

Why do you think it's exhibitionism?

CARL

I think it goes beyond simple ideas of performing, because there's no 'mask' being employed. There's nothing hidden. There's no pretending that you're having sex with someone when you are actually having sex with them.

LUCY

I think it's easier to think they're enjoying themselves, or they want us to enjoy ourselves. Why would you want to think about it so much? It's been made to turn you on, it's nothing deeper than that.

CARL

Really? You think that?

LUCY

Yeah, I do.

CARL

But . . . but when they're doing it, they're not lying. You can't say, 'I have an erection,' if you don't.

LUCY

There has to be some element of performance involved, Carl. What, they're *all* multi-orgasmic? They all love getting pounded like a catcher's mitt?

CARL

I thought you said you weren't bothered by it?

LUCY

I'm not. Or . . . I don't know. I've changed my mind. You've just seen a person change her mind.

CARL

Oh.

Beat.

LUCY

Carl, I can't have conversations like this any more.

CARL

You can't.

LUCY

I've met someone.

CARL

Oh.

LUCY

It's just not appropriate any more.

Beat.

CARL

You're right. I understand.

LUCY

I'm sorry.

CARL

No reason to be. You're showing absolute respect by being honest with me, instead of being weird or protracted about it. Thank you.

LUCY

You don't have to thank me.

CARL

Well, I'm just saying I like knowing where I stand. Otherwise I'd feel like a fool.

LUCY

All right.

A long beat.

CARL

What's her name?

Lucy looks up at him. He smiles at her. She smiles.

LUCY

He's an actor.

CARL

An actor.

A long beat. Carl looks like he's been shot in the stomach.

LUCY

You all right?

CARL

(*surprised*)

Hmm? (*recovering*) Thinking about the rest of the day. Jerry wants to see me.

LUCY

Really?

CARL

Mmm. (*Beat, thinking.*) The guy has never liked me. From day one. Nothing I can do. I think there are some hidden stairs and a secret handshake.

LUCY

I'm sure you'll do fine.

Beat.

CARL

Listen: what I heard, in your . . . *story*, was a lot of passion. And I think everyone should –

Cut.

INT. HOTEL KITCHEN. DAY.

Linda is taking a break. She is talking to her friend Mavis who works in room service.

LINDA

So there's this guy I met on the Internet.

MAVIS

Are we doing this now?

LINDA

He wants to meet me in Tucson for a weekend. He's a kid.

MAVIS

In Tucson? (*Exhales.*) Try these.

LINDA

Do they have sugar?

MAVIS

Sugar-free. Why Tucson?

LINDA

He lives near there.

MAVIS

A kid?

LINDA

Twenty-something.

MAVIS

And you're going?

LINDA

I think so.

MAVIS

He lives in the desert?

LINDA

We're staying in a Holiday Inn.

MAVIS

God.

LINDA

I'm intrigued.

MAVIS

In Tucson?

LINDA

These are good.

MAVIS

Sweetened with fruit juice. I could eat the whole tray.

LINDA

I bought new underwear.

MAVIS

Have you seen a photo?

LINDA

No.

MAVIS

The Holiday Inn part makes me sad.

LINDA

Why sad?

MAVIS

In Tucson?

LINDA

He knows a good one.

MAVIS

You've put some thought into this.

LINDA

Planned. We both have.

MAVIS

Like a wedding.

LINDA

Sort of.

Cut.

INT. LEE'S OFFICE. DAY.

Lee is reviewing Brian's papers. She is dressed conservatively but exudes a strong sexuality. Brian, forties, sits uncomfortably across from her. After a long silence she addresses him.

LEE

Mr Mimke.

BRIAN

Brian.

LEE

Brian. Funny, I dated a Randy Mimke in college.

BRIAN

Uh –

LEE

He had short legs and a great laugh.

BRIAN

Hmmm.

LEE

Preached to me about the evils of capitalism and performed satanic rituals on the football field after midnight.

BRIAN

My siblings' names all start with C.

LEE

Of course. Relax, Brian. This won't hurt, I promise.

BRIAN

I'm just –

Brian often shifts uncomfortably in his chair.

LEE

Mr Mimke, you've been with us for seven years, correct?

BRIAN

Right. Correct.

A beat.

LEE

You are aware of the recent . . . layoffs. Correct?

BRIAN

Well, yeah.

LEE

We're making some changes. Rearranging our priorities. Getting things straight. That sort of thing.

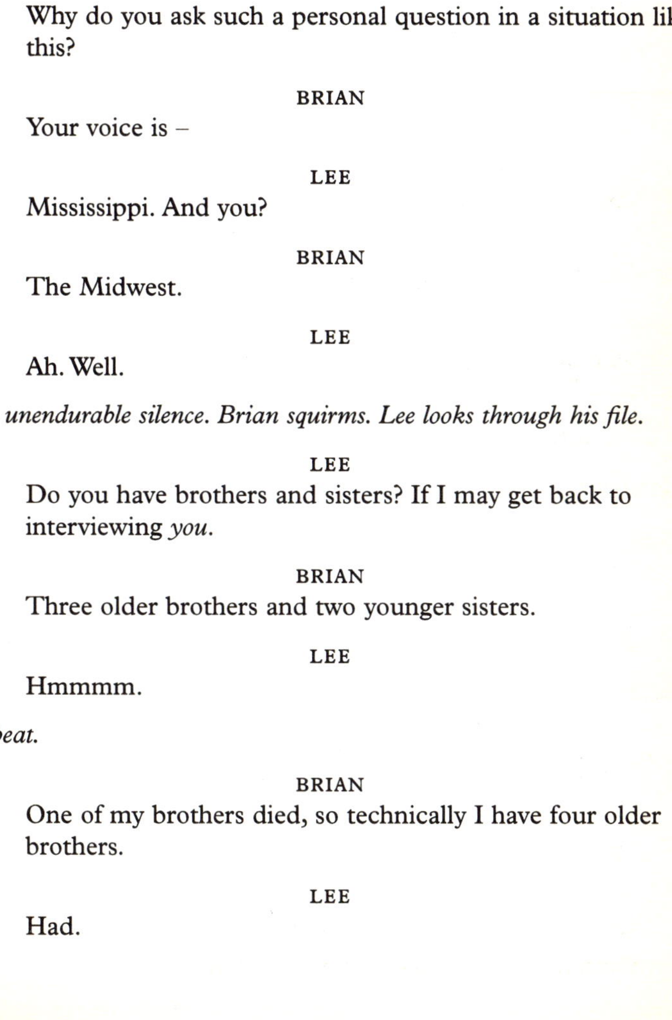

BRIAN

Where are you from?

LEE

Pardon?

BRIAN

Originally.

LEE

Why do you ask such a personal question in a situation like this?

BRIAN

Your voice is –

LEE

Mississippi. And you?

BRIAN

The Midwest.

LEE

Ah. Well.

An unendurable silence. Brian squirms. Lee looks through his file.

LEE

Do you have brothers and sisters? If I may get back to interviewing *you*.

BRIAN

Three older brothers and two younger sisters.

LEE

Hmmmm.

A beat.

BRIAN

One of my brothers died, so technically I have four older brothers.

LEE

Had.

BRIAN

Yes well, had.

LEE

How did he die?

BRIAN

Car accident.

LEE

How tragic.

BRIAN

An air bag would have saved him.

LEE

Hmmm.

BRIAN

If only –

LEE

Are you a smoker, Brian?

BRIAN

I participate when it's available.

LEE

Are you a smoker?

BRIAN

No. But I smoke –

LEE

Have you ever been caught driving under the influence?

BRIAN

Under the influence of what?

LEE

DUI – you are familiar with the term?

BRIAN

Yeah. No. What does this have to –

LEE

Do you vote Democrat or Republican?

BRIAN

Neither. Either. I vote for the best man.

LEE

And how do you judge that?

BRIAN

Well –

LEE

Do you know in an instant?

BRIAN

Yes.

LEE

Right. Hmmm.

Silence. She makes a note, then takes the beach ball out from under her desk.

Cut.

INT. PLANE. DAY.

Nicholas and Catherine (he's still eating).

CATHERINE

OK, this is worth noting.

NICHOLAS

I'm hungry.

CATHERINE

Um . . .

NICHOLAS

What? Are you one of those –

CATHERINE

What?

NICHOLAS

You don't eat?

CATHERINE

I can't eat airplane food.

NICHOLAS

What's wrong with it? This is first class. They cook this shit right on the premises.

CATHERINE

I'll wait for the cookies.

NICHOLAS

How corrupt was your father?

CATHERINE

And milk.

NICHOLAS

Did he kill people?

CATHERINE

He killed their spirits.

NICHOLAS

He threatened their identities.

CATHERINE

Something like that.

NICHOLAS

And what about you?

CATHERINE

He, uh –

NICHOLAS

You don't have to –

CATHERINE

No.

NICHOLAS

OK.

CATHERINE

I mean no, he didn't. He adored me.

NICHOLAS

Adored you. Huh. I don't think I've ever been adored.

CATHERINE

Could you elaborate?

NICHOLAS

Hold that thought.

Cut.

INT. PLANE BATHROOM. DAY.

Nicholas is sticking his fingers down his throat to make himself vomit. The ease with which it is done suggests that it is done often.

Cut.

INT. PLANE BATHROOM. DAY.

Nicholas, rinsing out his mouth, then popping a piece of gum.

Cut.

A VERY DIFFERENT SORT OF TITLE CARD, WITH MUSIC:

THE SOUND AND THE FÜHRER
by Arthur Dean.
ACT ONE, SCENE THREE

INT. THEATRE STAGE. DAY.

An actor, playing Hitler, smokes a cigarette and talks to an actress, presumably playing Eva Braun. She is sobbing.

A German officer stands to attention nearby.

HITLER

We've talked about this. Nothing has changed since the last time we had this discussion.

Beat.

I . . . I'm just too committed to my work to sustain a serious relationship right now.

Beat.

I bring the work home with me. You understand. I'm distracted. Then I hate myself for being distracted.

Beat.

You deserve better, believe me. I would only cause you pain.

Beat.

I'm doing you a favour. So be a nice girl or I'll have you thrown from the top of this building, OK?

She nods.

HITLER

Good. Off you go.

She leaves. Hitler exhales. To the guard, to the world:

HITLER

The four scariest words in the German language: 'We have to talk!'

Cut.

INT. HOTEL LOBBY. DAY.

Linda is talking to Lee on the cell phone.

LINDA

And today it was that redhead from his band or whatever. In the morning. It wasn't even nine.

LEE

You definitely have to move. You're obsessing.

LINDA

I can't afford to move. I'm waiting for him to move.

LEE

Oh, that's effective.

Beat.

Just meet us in the lobby. You'll have a great time and I know you'll love Gus.

LINDA

I have nothing to wear. I can't go to a party like that.

LEE

Wear that green dress. You look great in it.

LINDA

It doesn't fit me any more. And it has stains.

LEE

You always have an excuse.

LINDA

It's not an excuse, it's a reason. There's a difference.

LEE

Oh.

LINDA

Can we still have lunch? I have a birthday present for you.

LEE

It's tomorrow.

LINDA

I'm not here tomorrow.

LEE

You're breaking up, call me back.

Cut.

INT. PLANE. DAY.

Nicholas returns to his seat. Catherine is gone, he looks around, then figures she must be in the bathroom.

As he sits, he finds a card underneath him. Pulling it out from under his legs, he looks at it. 'Nicholas Turner' is typed on the front.

His brow furrows. He looks around. Was it . . . who might have left this? The sound of the bathroom door unlatching draws his attention. If it were Catherine, he wouldn't have time to open it, and so he begins to hide it until he sees that it isn't Catherine coming out of the bathroom. It's some businessman.

He turn his attention to the envelope and opens it swiftly. Inside is a typewritten letter. It reads: 'Nicholas, I will begin simply: I love you.'

There is more, but we don't see it. Instead, we see Nicholas's reaction to it, which is significant. In fact, upon finishing, he is well-nigh freaked out, though not necessarily in a bad way.

He leans his head back for a moment, trying to absorb it. Then he realises, whoever put this here is here. *Slowly he turns to look at the various women within sight.*

None of them looks back or give any indication that they might be the author of this letter, this declaration that has Nicholas so caught up.

The bathroom door opens, and Catherine emerges. Nicholas hides the letter and pulls out his magazine.

She sits, smiles, and pulls out her own magazine and begins to read.

Nicholas, now unable to read (if he ever was) because of curiosity, tries to sneak a look at her. Eventually he gives up and really gives reading a serious attempt.

And after, it seems he has actually begun to read:

NICHOLAS

Did you write it?

A blink from Catherine, then a look.

CATHERINE

Did I write what?

A scrutinising look from Nicholas, then a rueful head-shake.

NICHOLAS

Amazing. What a great fucking idea. Watch me squirm.

CATHERINE

What are you talking about?

NICHOLAS

Catherine.

CATHERINE

What are you talking about?

NICHOLAS

The letter.

CATHERINE

What letter?

He holds up the envelope with the letter inside.

CATHERINE

May I?

After a beat, he hands her the letter. She reads it. Her reaction is similar to his.

CATHERINE

This . . . it's pretty extraordinary.

Nicholas takes the letter back, looks at it for a moment, then rubs his face with his hand. Quietly:

NICHOLAS

Really, is this a prank? Just tell me.

CATHERINE

I don't think it's a prank.

NICHOLAS

So you didn't write it?

CATHERINE

Is it your fantasy that I wrote it?

NICHOLAS

Don't do that. It's not funny.

CATHERINE

I don't know what to tell you.

NICHOLAS

You cannot write about this.

CATHERINE

I can't?

NICHOLAS

No. It's not fair.

CATHERINE

It's human interest.

NICHOLAS

Interesting.

CATHERINE

It reveals your true character.

NICHOLAS

And yours.

CATHERINE

How so?

NICHOLAS

You're – you're good.

CATHERINE

They really do have ovens back there.

NICHOLAS

I'm on to you.

CATHERINE

Uh – I think I'm on to *you*.

NICHOLAS

Look at me.

She looks at him.

NICHOLAS

Did you write that letter?

Catherine looks out the window.

NICHOLAS

Yeah. See?

Catherine looks suddenly back at Nicholas.

CATHERINE

I don't want to play this game any more with you.

She picks up her magazine and starts to read. Nicholas rips up the letter to see what her reaction will be. She looks at him and smiles. He stuffs it into Catherine's seat-pouch. She ignores him.

Cut.

INT. HOTEL LOBBY. DAY.

Linda is talking to Lee on her cell phone.

LEE

You're flying?

LINDA

Yeah.

LEE

When?

LINDA

I told you. Tomorrow.

LEE

Right.

LINDA

You're not being very supportive.

LEE

I'm just trying to –

LINDA

Just be happy for me.

LEE

Happy for you?

Silence.

LINDA

I knew you'd take this road.

LEE

Then why did you tell me? Why didn't you spring it on me after you'd spent a weekend with this young desert buck? Why didn't you wait until you could show me the polaroids from your dingy little room at the Holiday Inn?

LINDA

I wouldn't show you.

LEE

Then don't tell me.

LINDA

You do this.

LEE

What?

LINDA

Judge me.

LEE

I'm not judging you. I have to go. Lunch today, then. Party tonight.

Cut.

INT. HOTEL ROOM. DAY.

Linda is talking to a middle-aged woman, Diane, that she is massaging. Diane has nice shit.

LINDA

I'm just there to get a regular check-up, no big deal. And he is the most respected doctor in the city, OK? Fifties, very distinguished, obviously successful. So he's telling me this and that about my results, which are normal, and then he starts . . . he starts talking like a madman. Not like his voice gets weird, but he starts saying things that are totally crazy, like crazy racist shit about different ethnic groups, but he's saying it in this totally normal tone of voice. So I'm not sure what to do, and I'm feeling really uncomfortable and I want to get out of there, but then he starts telling me that he can make me invisible. And this I am suddenly interested in. And I let him strap me in this chair and he starts to give me this drip that will make me invisible.

DIANE

When I was in a band I had dreams like that all the time. Are you friends with your mother?

LINDA

Sort of. When I got older she confessed that she used to hear voices as a girl and hoped that she didn't hand that down to me.

DIANE

What about your father?

LINDA

He died when I was ten.

DIANE

Were you very close?

Beat.

LINDA

Well, I was ten.

DIANE

Mine divorced my mother and starting asking me if he could date my friends.

Cut.

INT. OFFICE. DAY.

Carl and a colleague.

CARL

I'll tell you why: I saw a show the other night, and there was an interview with a guy that just turned one hundred years old, and he had a full head of hair. A *hundred*. I'm fucking forty-one. I know, it's not like facing death in the jungles of Vietnam, but it's a low-level sort of free-floating anxiety. I have anxiety about it. Homeless guys, for Christ's sake. Homeless guys with hair send me into a rage. I mean . . .?

COLLEAGUE

And you think Lee minds?

CARL

She says no. Actually, that's a lie: she doesn't say anything. I assume that's a no. We don't connect. We sit in the same room. We live in the same house. But –

COLLEAGUE

And.

CARL

What?

COLLEAGUE

Try changing your buts to ands. See what happens.

Carl thinks about that.

CARL

We live in the same house *and* –

COLLEAGUE

See?

Cut.

INT. LEE'S OFFICE. DAY.

Lee is about to give bad news to another guy. She is in the early stages of blowing up the same beach ball from the previous scene.

LEE

Have you ever been to Europe?

DAVID

Are you kidding?

LEE

Just answer the questions, Mr Addlington – David.

DAVID

Yes. Of course I've been to Europe. Shall I name the countries?

LEE

Not yet.

Silence. Lee takes him in visually. David tries to remain calm.

DAVID

Did you really kill a deer?

LEE

That's what I said. Would you say you are someone who takes an initiative?

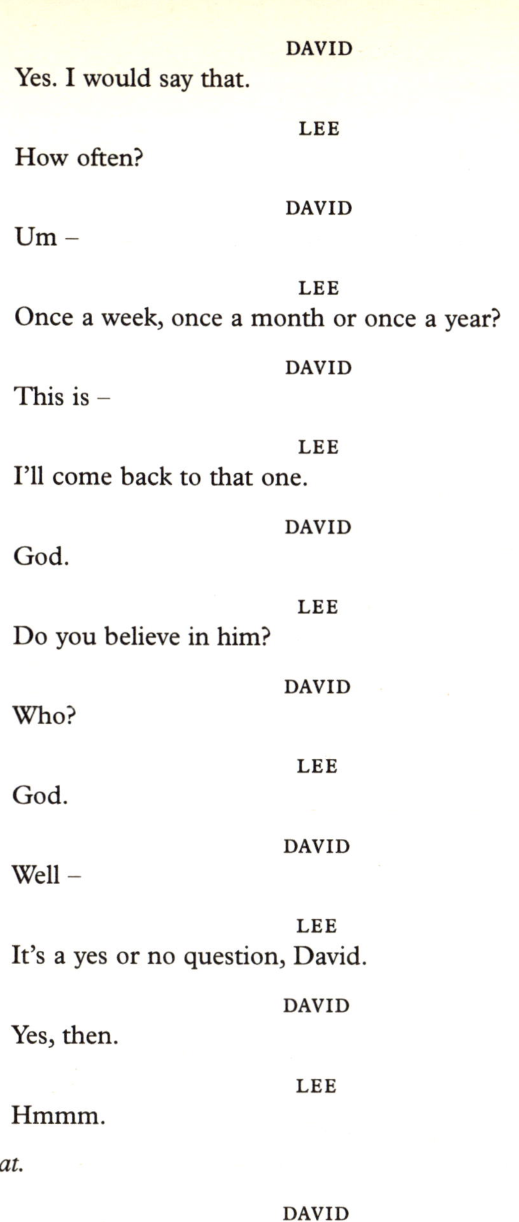

DAVID

Yes. I would say that.

LEE

How often?

DAVID

Um –

LEE

Once a week, once a month or once a year?

DAVID

This is –

LEE

I'll come back to that one.

DAVID

God.

LEE

Do you believe in him?

DAVID

Who?

LEE

God.

DAVID

Well –

LEE

It's a yes or no question, David.

DAVID

Yes, then.

LEE

Hmmm.

A beat.

DAVID

I mean, no.

LEE

Are you undecided?

DAVID

I thought this was –

LEE

You seem to be a very generous person.

DAVID

Thank you –

LEE

And wise.

DAVID

Hmmm.

LEE

I'll be straight with you.

DAVID

Um.

LEE

In three years, you haven't impressed a single person in this agency. I've asked everyone about your performance, right down to the night cleaning crew. They all think you're worthless.

DAVID

I see.

LEE

You'll be notified officially through the mail.

DAVID

I'll watch for it.

LEE

Do you have a girlfriend?

DAVID

What?

LEE

Are you involved?

Lee opens the window behind her and lights a cigarette.

DAVID

Are you . . . are you? What are you doing?

LEE

Put that chair against the door.

DAVID

You're kidding. I think I should –

LEE

Then stand on the chair balanced on one leg.

A very long pause.

DAVID

Ms Bright. Is this a joke?

LEE

This is a test of skill, of sorts. I like you. I'll tell you that right now.

Beat.

DAVID

Do you mind if I take off my shoes?

LEE

Why?

DAVID

For balance.

LEE

OK. And when you're ready, just put that chair against the door.

DAVID

OK.

David puts the chair by the door. He advances towards her in a seductive way. She has finished blowing up the beach ball now.

LEE

Stand on the chair.

DAVID

What?

LEE

On one leg. Balanced.

DAVID

You're a piece of work. You know that?

David takes off his shoes and stands balanced on one leg. Lee throws him the beach ball. She continues to toss it to him as she fires her questions and responses.

LEE

Name the countries in Africa.

DAVID

This is –

LEE

You have one minute.

Cut.

INT. HOTEL HALLWAY. DAY.

Linda, carrying her massage table, makes her way to a client's room. En route, she passes a man on his hands and knees. He is scurrying in the opposite direction and counting doors as he goes. Linda looks back at him and for a brief moment he stops to look back at her before returning to his task.

INT. HOTEL ROOM. DAY.

Linda is massaging a very old woman.

WOMAN

You're touch is electric.

LINDA

I can't even feel what I'm touching any more.

WOMAN

Could you focus on my feet this time?

LINDA

I think about the future a lot.

WOMAN

The future is Spanish.

Cut.

INT. PLANE. DAY.

Catherine is sleeping. Nicholas retrieves the torn-up letter from her seat-pouch. She wakes up from her nap.

NICHOLAS

You were gone.

CATHERINE

What time is it?

Beat.

I feel nauseous.

NICHOLAS

Who are you to me?

CATHERINE

Look, I think you're very talented and interesting. I'm probably going to write a kick-ass piece about you, but you are really pissing me off about that letter.

NICHOLAS

No. You are pissing me off.

They are both stunned by this exchange. They are silenced by it.

Cut.

INT. HOTEL. DAY.

Linda is massaging a male client. Sounds of violent sex from the next room start to beat like a drum. It is really loud. Linda turns up the tape of ocean sounds she has put in.

CLIENT

Can you turn that down a little?

LINDA

Sorry.

The sounds are still thumping and loud. Then a silence followed by the drone of a TV.

CLIENT

I like it hard.

LINDA

Is this hard enough?

CLIENT

You could go a little deeper.

LINDA

Tell me when it hurts.

CLIENT

I don't think you could – ow –

LINDA

There?

CLIENT

– hurt me.

LINDA

There's memory stored here.

CLIENT

What?

LINDA

Memory. Just breathe.

CLIENT

You're good.

LINDA

Thank you.

CLIENT

What was your name again?

LINDA

Ann.

CLIENT

Well, Ann, you're a strong girl. Oh my God.

LINDA

Breathe.

The client lets out a loud exhalation/groan.

Cut.

INT. OFFICE. DAY.

Carl is leaning in the doorway of a new colleague, Tracy, at work. She is young and attractive.

CARL

Your porn name is your middle name and the street you lived on in high school.

TRACY

I've really got to –

CARL

I'm Andrew Highland.

TRACY

Um.

CARL

Middle name. You're Tracy

TRACY

I don't have a middle name.

CARL

OK, I think you can use the name of your first pet.

TRACY

We didn't have pets.

Cut.

INT. LAX AIRPORT. DAY.

Nicholas, on the phone. Catherine stands a slight distance away. After a long beat of intense listening:

NICHOLAS

In talks? What the fuck? In *talks*.

Beat.

I need this.

Beat.

All right.

He hangs up.

Cut.

EXT. TOWN CAR. DAY.

NICHOLAS

I have a friend who grew up in Iran, moved here in '75 and hasn't been back. He told me that at a certain point he realised that he was thinking in English, his interior monologue had changed to English, and not long after that he started to dream in English.

CATHERINE

That makes sense. The conscious first, then the unconscious.

NICHOLAS

Why do you say that?

CATHERINE

Well, I think language is a superficial way of communicating when compared to something like the subconscious. Our conscious selves would submit sooner, be tricked earlier.

NICHOLAS

Language is a trick? What, Shakespeare and *Death of a Salesman*? People have used language to express some pretty significant subconscious emotions. Are you saying we should just walk around in a dream state all the time? That's fucking flaky.

CATHERINE

Oops. Pressed a button.

NICHOLAS

What, somebody who acts on television can't be passionate about something? I must be cardboard if I do this for a living? There are people out there who get something from these shows. Why would they be watching if they didn't? I hear from some of them.

CATHERINE

OK.

A long beat.

NICHOLAS

I wish I hadn't said that.

CATHERINE

Why?

NICHOLAS

I would really feel exposed if you printed that I said that.

CATHERINE

Why?

Cut.

INT. LEE'S OFFICE. DAY.

Lee is talking to a woman. Or rather, she is throwing the woman the beach ball and asking her questions.

ARLENE

I –

LEE

Do you know the countries in Africa, Arlene?

ARLENE

Algeria.

LEE

A great starting point.

ARLENE

Tanzania.

LEE

Interesting.

ARLENE

Sudan.

LEE

Hmmm.

ARLENE

Nigeria.

LEE

Take your time. Breathe. Relax. Have some fun.

ARLENE

Ivory Coast, Senegal, Sierra Leone –

LEE

Hmmm.

ARLENE

Ghana.

LEE

Have you ever been convicted of a crime?

Arlene shakes her head, 'No'.

ARLENE

Mali.

LEE

Have you been tested lately for the HIV virus?

Arlene shakes her head, 'No', then, 'Yes'.

ARLENE

Zaire.

LEE

Have you ever been married?

Arlene shakes her head.

ARLENE

Egypt. Morocco. Mozambique. Angola.

LEE

Very good.

ARLENE

Emma.

LEE

Not a country.

ARLENE

My sister.

LEE

Keep going.

ARLENE

Twice.

LEE

You're being timed – I know you are clever.

ARLENE

Congo.

LEE

Stay there.

ARLENE

Cameroon.

LEE

God, you're good.

ARLENE

Gabon. Angola.

LEE

You've already said that.

ARLENE

Zaire.

LEE

Go east.

ARLENE

Kenya.

LEE

Oh God, yes.

ARLENE

Somali Republic.

LEE

Shit. Keep going.

ARLENE

Ethiopia.

LEE

Time. You are very impressive.

ARLENE

I don't think you're allowed to do this.

LEE

Of course I am. Get down from there.

Cut.

INT. LEE'S CAR. DAY.

Lee gets in and starts the car.

Cut.

INT. LEE'S CAR. DAY.

Lee drives really fast down a freeway.

Cut.

INT. JERRY'S OFFICE. DAY.

Carl talks.

CARL

My friend Gus says that the straight world will always be fascinated by gangster sagas, because here are people who say, 'We are not going to live by an unspoken rule that I don't take you to the cleaners when you're not looking. We don't have an agreement that I will not take advantage of you.' They're in the minority – they have to be, or sheer anarchy would ensue – and we love watching them. It's a walk on the wild side, with no real risk of corruption. It's two-dimensional. And it will always be compelling. Sometimes we can't look away, and we should.

Beat. Jerry enters. We realise Carl has been talking to no one.

JERRY

Hey, Carl, how you doin', pal?

CARL

Good. I'm good, Jerry, thanks.

JERRY

Great.

Cut.

EXT. HOTEL PATIO. DAY.

Linda and Lee are eating lunch by the pool.

LINDA

I keep bringing it up because I don't want you to think I've forgotten.

LEE

Well, I don't want half. Just pay me back when you have all of it.

LINDA

I don't know when that will be. I have half now.

LEE

Keep it. Pay me when you have the whole thing.

LINDA

But I –

LEE

Are you still going on your dirty little weekend with that guy from the Internet? Don't you need money for that?

LINDA

At least I'm putting myself out there.

LEE

Guess so.

LINDA

Meeting men.

LEE

On the Internet? How is that meeting?

LINDA

Encountering.

LEE

Masturbation.

LINDA

Trust.

LEE

Bullshit.

LINDA

Something you know nothing about.

LEE

I believe in fate as much as you do. Make a list. Which airline are you flying?

LINDA

Southwest.

LEE

Southwest, younger man, new underwear, Tucson, Holiday Inn.

LINDA

What's your point?

LEE

Have you ever stayed in a Holiday Inn?

LINDA

Have you?

LEE

I think that's what's really bothering me.

LINDA

He's paying for it.

LEE

That's even worse, what does he do?

LINDA

An artist.

LEE

An actor?

LINDA

A painter.

LEE

In *Tucson*?

LINDA

He says the desert inspires him.

LEE

Is that what you talk – type about?

LINDA

Look, I'm feeling really exposed and raw right now. You're asking too many questions. I've just met a guy, all right?

LEE

That's great.

LINDA

On the Internet.

LEE

How modern.

LINDA

And you?

Beat.

LEE

And me what?

Cut.

TITLE CARD, WITH MUSIC:

ACT TWO, SCENE ONE.

INT. THEATRE STAGE. DAY.

The actor playing Hitler is sitting in the back of a car. An attractive young girl is sitting next to him.

HITLER

It's not safe to hitchhike around here, you know.

Beat.

You're lucky I came along.

Beat.

I just have to do this rally thing. Say a few words.

Beat.

You can watch from the stage.

Beat.

Then maybe you and I can go somewhere and have a few words of our own.

Beat.

I'm very interested in young people, their ideas. They're invigorating, young people.

Beat.

In fact, you've given me an idea. I will speak about young people tonight. About how they can contribute. Yes.

Beat.

You see, you have inspired me. A young person has inspired me.

Beat.

I knew it.

Cut.

INT. OFFICE. DAY.

Carl is talking to Jerry.

CARL

I think that's worth discussing. I really do.

JERRY

Carl, you've got a good mind. And by God, you've got a lot to say. Someone down in sales said you sold a screenplay that you co-wrote with your friend –

CARL

Arty, he's my –

JERRY

That's fantastic. That's really fantastic. It's a home run, kid. You know what the odds of that are, Carl? How many people try to sell screenplays? That's great. You're on your way.

CARL

Well, I still enjoy –

JERRY

Enjoy it.

CARL

Yes, thank you.

JERRY

We're proud of you.

CARL

But –

JERRY

But let me ask you a question: when you're at home, and you get a beer from the refrigerator, do you pour it into a glass, or do you drink it from the bottle?

Beat.

CARL

I pour it into a glass.

JERRY

Exactly. You see, Carl: I want this magazine to drink out of the bottle.

Cut.

EXT. HOTEL PATIO. DAY.

Lee and Linda are still eating lunch. Linda looks at people coming and going.

LINDA

Fuck, marry or murder?

LEE

This is my mother, when I was four, introducing me to people: 'And this is Lee. She ruined my body, didn't you, dear?'

Beat.

LINDA

Is that why you're always Joey Heatherton on Halloween?

Lee looks at her.

LINDA

It's a great costume – really. If Joey herself happens to come by and actually recognises it.

She returns to the game.

Fuck, marry or murder?

LEE

I really hate this game.

LINDA

For fun.

LEE

They *all* seem so violent.

LINDA

And possible.

LEE

You're so glib.

LINDA

What?

LEE

Tomorrow's my birthday.

LINDA

Can't we play a fun game in honour of your birthday?

LEE

I think it's childish. Like that gift you gave me last year on my birthday.

LINDA

What did I give you?

LEE

On my fortieth birthday.

LINDA

You make forty a bigger deal than it is.

LEE

You have no idea about forty.

LINDA

I'll be forty some day.

LEE

Fuck you.

LINDA

Fifty, even.

Silence.

LINDA

So what did I give you?

LEE

The, you know. The blue thing, orange juicer – like jello.

LINDA

The pleasure dome? You thought that was childish?

LEE

I would have rather had just a card. Now take Gus, this guy knows how to give a gift. Last year he gave me a first edition of Bernard Shaw's *The Sanity of Art*.

LINDA

Do you use it?

LEE

Which?

LINDA

The present I gave you.

LEE

Are you kidding?

LINDA

No?

LEE

But for my fortieth birthday?

LINDA

Something fun.

LEE

I was offended.

LINDA

I have one.

LEE

I used it once.

LINDA

What happened?

LEE

I got stuck in the chair.

LINDA

You used it in a chair?

LEE

Well, that's what's on the box.

LINDA

The model?

LEE

Well how do you use it?

LINDA

Different ways.

LEE

But on my fortieth birthday?

LINDA

I thought you'd think it was funny.

LEE

Gift-giving is an art.

Silence.

Someone walks by and distracts Linda.

LINDA

Fuck, marry or murder?

LEE

You should have the person in mind at all times.

Linda follows this person with her eyes.

LINDA

Definitely fuck.

LEE

You should give people what you think they would want.

LINDA

I thought you'd like it.

LEE

Something personal.

LINDA

Personal?

LEE

I'm just saying how it felt. And then you know, you came to the party but you and that guy, what was his name? Tom? –

you sat at the other end of the table and stared at each other the whole time. You didn't even really socialise with anyone else.

LINDA

Oh God forgive me, I was in love for a brief period of time that happened to include the week of your birthday. A year later. This is all a year later. Oh, before I forget – happy birthday to you.

Linda takes a small box out of her bag and hands it to Lee.

Silence.

LINDA

And you know, a gift is a gift. You shouldn't question it – at least not out loud and to the giver and a whole year later.

LEE

Now I know.

LINDA

What?

LEE

That it meant something to you.

LINDA

What?

LEE

The whole thing. That you *did* put some thought into it.

There is a silence between them. Lee opens the box and finds a change purse in the shape of a sock. Lee is speechless and looks at Linda.

LINDA

It's for your – you know – small change.

Lee thinks about that.

Cut.

EXT. CAFE. DAY.

Nicholas and Catherine are standing on the set of Nicholas's TV show.

CATHERINE

Then he gives me this injection, and I become invisible. And I can do anything, right, I'm invisible? What do I do? I go to one of my colleagues, Carl, and I make him sign a confession while I hold a knife to his neck.

Beat.

It's just weird, because I actually like Carl. He's a brilliant, talented man. Completely misunderstood by his boss. I'm not surprised he was in my dream because I think of him a lot. Sometimes I think I'm actually –

AD'S VOICE

Nicholas, we're ready for you.

He smiles at Catherine.

NICHOLAS

I want to tell you what I think about that, but . . .

CATHERINE

I'll be here.

Nicholas takes his mark next to Huge White Male Movie Star. The camera rolls, the take begins, and the two men jog toward the camera capturing their actions.

NICHOLAS

(*in character as the sidekick*)

Looks like we're too late.

HUGE WHITE MALE MOVIE STAR

Looks like.

NICHOLAS

Back to square one.

HUGE WHITE MALE MOVIE STAR

That's what he thinks.

NICHOLAS

You think different?

HUGE WHITE MALE MOVIE STAR

I know different. Come on.

The Huge White Male Movie Star jogs off his mark. Nicholas exhales dramatically and then follows.

DIRECTOR

And we cut. Great. Great, Brad.

Moments later:

Nicholas is with Catherine. His expression says: 'Hey, what can I do?'

CATHERINE

Would you not take a role if you thought people in the black community wouldn't like it?

A beat.

NICHOLAS

There's a guy in my neighbourhood, right across the street. And this guy is dressed as a vampire twenty-four hours a day. I don't know anything about him, don't know if he has a job, all I know is that he dresses like Dracula all the time. I've seen him at Pavilions, buying romaine lettuce, dressed like Dracula. Now, he's an actor, right? Must have been an actor?

Catherine shrugs.

CATHERINE

You could find out.

NICHOLAS

The answer to your question is: if I needed the money, yes.

She looks at him. He shrugs. Then, suddenly, he looks at the camera, at us, as if to say: 'OK, are we done here?'

DIRECTOR

Cut it. Great. Let's eat.

We reveal we are watching a movie within a movie. Nicholas is being played by Calvin and Catherine by Francesca.

A general sense of relief and film-set activity breaks out. Sound technicians descend on Calvin and Francesca to remove their wireless microphones. Within seconds, Francesca has an assistant hovering nearby with bottled water and a cell phone. As Francesca is about to be led away:

CALVIN

Could you –

FRANCESCA

What?

CALVIN

Could you give me a little more to work with on the attraction thing?

FRANCESCA

What do you mean?

CALVIN

I mean, I thought it was building and in this scene you were just all back to no feeling.

FRANCESCA

Really. Huh. Well, are you eating, because we could –

CALVIN

No, I've got to run an errand.

Beat.

I don't know. We'll figure it out. Maybe it's me.

Cut.

INT. HOTEL. DAY.

Calvin passes Linda in the lobby.

Cut.

EXT. ROOM 203. DAY.

Calvin knocks. The door opens sightly.

CALVIN

Lee. Hey, I –

She grabs him, pulls him inside, and shuts the door.

Cut.

INT. ROOM 203. DAY.

Calvin goes down on Lee.

LEE

Oh, God. Calvin, really focus. I only have an hour.

Cut.

INT. ROOM 203. DAY.

Lee in Calvin's arms. Afterwards. Naked. He looks a little distracted.

LEE

I show up at a dinner party, well dressed, bottle of gift wine in hand –

CALVIN

Alone?

LEE

Yes. And when the door opens I can see the look of shock and horror on the host's face – her smile just slides right onto the floor. She is literally paralysed by the embarrassment she's feeling for me. I look around, noticing everyone present. I recognise all of them; of course I would attend a gathering of these people. On another occasion this event might have been put together for me.

CALVIN

Likc a birthday.

LEE

Right. The host has unfrozen herself and has me by the elbow before I can even register everyone who has come to the party. And then she hisses at me: 'You can't be here. You're dead.' And when I look to the guests I know that she is right. No one can hold my stare. See, I knew something was wrong, but I didn't know it was that.

Beat.

I had that one this morning.

Beat.

CALVIN

I need to talk to you about something.

Cut.

Lee is sitting in chair, half-dressed. She looks stunned.

CALVIN

Lee –

LEE

Don't. Look, it just must be a rhythm thing, you know? Like when the windshield wipers on the bus start flopping towards each other or – like when you think someone said, 'You're really beautiful,' when what they actually said was, 'Does beer make you full?'

Calvin's cell phone rings. He looks to see who's calling. He lets it ring until it stops.

Cut.

Beat.

CALVIN

You came and spoke to me. This began because of you.

LEE

Are you saying you weren't attracted to me?

CALVIN

You were *married. Are* married.

LEE

Gus told me to watch out for you.

CALVIN

He told me to watch out for you.

Cut.

LEE

You talk like you're stoned.

Cut.

I'm forty-one tomorrow, Calvin. My hair is thinning, gravity is like, out of control. I'm at the age when I can have a stroke in the middle of the night or –

Calvin clears his throat and starts to say something.

LEE

I left Carl a letter this morning, saying basically that I don't want to be married any more.

Calvin looks at her, struck by the coincidence.

LEE

If you think I'm not going to Gus's because . . . well, it's shocking. I thought we had more than that, that's all. Go fuck somebody else. I have a meeting.

Cut.

INT. TRAILER. DAY.

Francesca is unwrapping a sandwich. Her assistant is sitting across from her.

ASSISTANT

Tuna. No celery.

Francesca nods and takes a bite.

ASSISTANT

So listen, that thing we were talking about? I can't keep . . . I mean, this is . . . I'm uncomfortable dealing with this aspect of your life.

FRANCESCA

Well, I don't want to talk to them.

ASSISTANT

Well I don't want to talk to them, either. I don't even want to talk to the guys *I'm* dating.

FRANCESCA

I'm not dating them. A single date is not dating.

ASSISTANT

Well, somebody buys you dinner, you owe them a phone call, in my opinion.

FRANCESCA

See, dinner. That's where I fucked up. It should've been lunch. Lunch is meaningless.

A beat.

ASSISTANT

They all seemed pretty nice to me.

FRANCESCA

You don't think they had that 'I wanna be able to say I fucked Francesca Davis' thing going?

ASSISTANT

So date guys you knew before you were famous.

FRANCESCA

They're all taken.

Cut.

INT. HOTEL. DAY.

Lee walks through the hotel and passes Linda.

LINDA

Hey.

Lee is startled and turns around.

LEE

Hi.

LINDA

You're still here?

LEE

I was shopping for my friend Gus.

LINDA

Oh.

Lee is clearly upset, but Linda is unsure how to broach the subject.

LEE

I've . . . I've had some very sad cases today.

LINDA

Oh. I'm sorry.

LEE

It's emotional.

LINDA

What'd you get him?

LEE

Who?

LINDA

Gus.

LEE

They didn't have it.

LINDA

What is it?

LEE

It's a – thing – that – well he's forty. And . . .

LINDA

Lee.

LEE

I have to go.

Linda watches Lee exit the lobby onto the street. Linda passes Calvin again. He checks her out as she passes. We follow Calvin out.

Cut.

Title card, with music:

ACT THREE, SCENE THREE.

INT. THEATRE STAGE. DAY.

Hitler is lifting weights. Goebbels watches, along with a few guards.

HITLER

I used to go to the gym, but it was too social. People coming up to me, interrupting. Then, if I happened to speak to a young lady, everybody's saying, 'Oh, look, Hitler's talking to so-and-so.' Who needs that? It's childish. So then I thought: I'll just have a little space built here, nothing fancy.'

Beat.

I get depressed when I don't exercise.

Beat.

These moods descend on me, these black moods. Last September, I sprained my knee a little, doing lunges, you know, and I had to stay off it for three weeks. Ugh. All during Poland I was depressed.

Cut.

EXT. CAR. DAY.

Nicholas and Catherine.

CATHERINE

If you have to make a serial-killer movie, I think it's a pretty good one. A lot of it will be in the execution. Ed's a good writer?

NICHOLAS

Yeah. I saw some one-acts that he wrote, and we've been working together.

CATHERINE

You pay him?

NICHOLAS

Yeah, I mean. Well, he acts, too, once in a while. All right: off the record?

CATHERINE

Sure.

NICHOLAS

I give him three grand a month, and we work on stuff. But if you wrote that, I mean, he has –

CATHERINE

I understand.

Cut.

INT. OFFICE. DAY.

Nicholas and his writing partner (Ed) sit and wait for their meeting. Catherine sits with them.

ED

And then I pee green. I go to the bathroom, and my pee is green, like pickle juice.

NICHOLAS

Jesus.

ED

Weird, right?

NICHOLAS

You should write them down.

Beat.

ED

Yeah, maybe.

Beat. Catherine and Nicholas exchange looks.

Cut.

INT. OFFICE. DAY.

Nicholas and Ed are pitching to Harvey Weinstein and some studio executives. Catherine sits off in the corner, taking notes.

NICHOLAS

We open with this guy, watching TV as he gets ready to go to work. He sees a murder described, and as he's listening, his face goes fucking *white* and he bolts out of his apartment. We follow him, racing in his car, racing downtown, racing to . . . the police station. He bluffs his way into seeing the lead detective and tells him: 'That murder I saw described on TV, that's a murder I wrote in a book, a piece of fiction, a few years ago.' They say bullshit, and he reels off this list of facts –

ED

– that nobody knows but the police.

The executives look at Harvey, who just stares at Nicholas and Ed.

NICHOLAS

(*'don't fucking interrupt'*)

Right. So he's obviously telling the truth. So, he begins to predict what will happen –

ED

– and all of it comes true.

These words scroll across the bottom of the screen:

THIS TAPE FOR SCREENING PURPOSES ONLY.
DO NOT SELL OR RENT.

NICHOLAS

Except one thing. The murders deviate at a key point, for reasons no one can understand, because up to this point the killer has followed this author's book to the letter. So the detective is confused, he calls the author and tells him, hey, this doesn't seem right, in the book it said this, but the murderer did something different.

ED

'What did he do?' the author asks the detective.

NICHOLAS

And the detective begins to tell him, and this weird look comes over the writer's face. Then there's a long pause, and the author says, 'I was going to write that, but changed it during some revisions. I was going to write exactly that, it's in early versions of the manuscript.' And the detective says, 'Great, then it must be someone who had access to one of these manuscripts. You got a list?' 'Yeah,' the writer says. 'Me.' And he hangs up the phone.

HARVEY

The author is the killer.

NICHOLAS

Right.

They nod.

ED

We were thinking, one thing was the murder victims have a symbol carved into their skin that the killer has as a tattoo.

The execs just stare.

HARVEY

(*encouraging them*)

This sounds like something Bob would like.

Cut.

EXT. PARKING LOT. DAY.

Nicholas and Ed (*and Catherine, of course*).

NICHOLAS

Motherfuckers. Watching them look at us, their faces. Like labradors staring at a Picasso.

ED

Yeah.

NICHOLAS

We went in there with a china cup, these people want beer mugs.

ED

Yeah, right.

NICHOLAS

And I could so see me in that part.

ED

(*not quickly*)

Right.

NICHOLAS

Fuck. All right. Talk to you later.

ED

OK.

NICHOLAS

Keep the faith.

Cut.

INT. CARL'S OFFICE. DAY.

Carl is being consoled by Lucy.

CARL

One minute I'm pouring a beer, the next minute I'm unemployed. How did this happen? How did the act of pouring hops into a glass in the privacy of my home get me fired? He said I've confused my personality quirks with standards. What the fuck?

Lucy looks at him, sympathetic. A male colleague sticks his head in the door, trying to cheer Carl up.

COLLEAGUE

Carl. You hear about Thomas Edison?

CARL

No, what?

COLLEAGUE

Dead. Heart attack.

With the deadpan perfect timing of a rim shot, the colleague ducks away. Carl and Lucy smile. Then:

LUCY

I don't know. Take some time off. Learn a language.

CARL

I know a language.

She looks at him staring off into space.

LUCY

Do the thing for me.

CARL

What thing?

LUCY

You know, the phone thing.

CARL

Not now.

LUCY

Please, Carl.

CARL

All right.

Carl swallows and then speaks. When he does, his voice sounds exactly like it's coming over a telephone line.

CARL

Thank you for calling Moviefone. If the title you selected is –

Lucy laughs hysterically.

CARL

(*still doing the phone voice*)

Why is that so funny to you?

Cut.

EXT. HOTEL ROOM. DAY.

Linda knocks on Room 205. A gorgeous man, Gus, wearing a robe, answers the door.

LINDA

Mr Liveright?

GUS

Bill. Come in. Ann?

LINDA

Bill Liveright. Great name.

Linda shakes his hand and goes in with her table.

Cut.

LATER, IN ROOM 205.

Linda is massaging Gus.

LINDA

. . . this drip that will make me invisible.

GUS

You're not connecting.

LINDA

What do you mean?

GUS

It means you're afraid of really connecting. You're relieved when you can disappear.

LINDA

But why does he have to strap me in the chair?

GUS

Oh come on, Ann, we all like to be strapped down. Something to push against.

LINDA

You think so?

Cut.

Title card: 'One minute later.'

Cut.

INT. HOTEL. DAY.

Linda is massaging Gus' feet.

LINDA

It has just always eluded me.

GUS

Money is just feminine energy.

LINDA

It seems so male. I don't get it.

GUS

Mater – money. Connect with that and you're golden.

LINDA

You make it seem so simple.

GUS

It is.

LINDA

Just connecting with it.

GUS

Right. You're catching on. Listen, don't be one of the confused people. Some people are so confused, even if they could figure out whether or not to blame someone, they wouldn't know who to blame. So if you have clarity, if you have purpose, you can wade right through. It's like running past people who are asleep.

LINDA

You can turn over now.

There is an awkward silence, during which Gus gets an erection under the sheet. Linda tries to ignore it.

GUS

You from LA?

LINDA

I am, actually.

Beat.

You?

GUS

New York. I lived here, though.

LINDA

How long?

GUS

A day.

LINDA

A day?

GUS

A day. I had actually moved to Los Angeles, bought a house, the whole thing. The evening of the first day, I go to a dinner party. About ten minutes after I'm there, I overhear somebody say, 'My ex-drug dealer is running for Prime Minister of Belgium.' I took the first flight back the next morning.

Linda smiles, still ignoring his erection. She massages a bit too hard.

GUS

That hurts, actually.

LINDA

Sorry.

More awkward silence between them. Linda's ocean tape cannot save her.

GUS

Ann?

LINDA

Bill.

GUS

Ann, it's my birthday.

LINDA

Really? Happy birthday.

GUS

What is your philosophy on release?

LINDA

Um. Look, Bill, I know where you're going with this and I don't do that.

GUS

Not even for a bit of extra cash?

LINDA

I am a masseuse, Bill, and not that kind of masseuse. The release I offer is a release of toxins – a release of tension – and sometimes a release of emotions.

GUS

Yes.

LINDA

I can't. I'll be fired.

GUS

It would take thirty seconds.

LINDA

You can come in thirty seconds?

GUS

Do you have a second hand?

LINDA

In fact I do.

GUS

You can stop after thirty seconds.

LINDA

I can't.

GUS

For five hundred dollars? When was the last time you made five hundred dollars in thirty seconds?

LINDA

You're cruel.

GUS

I'm practical. You need the cash and I need the release.

LINDA

This is –

GUS

Five hundred dollars in cash.

Linda thinks about this.

LINDA

You can't make any noise.

GUS

Release is noisy.

LINDA

You can audibly exhale but you can't moan or sigh or grunt.

GUS

No noise – just audibly exhale –

Gus exhales loudly.

LINDA

Not that loud.

GUS

Ready? Five hundred.

LINDA

Fuck.

GUS

Go.

Cut.

Title card: 'Forty seconds later.'

Cut.

INT. HOTEL BATHROOM. DAY.

Linda is in the bathroom washing her hands. She looks over at the toilet and does a double-take. She walks over to confirm what she's seen: the water in the toilet is green. *Backing away, she knocks Gus/Bill's pants from the door. Curious, she reaches into one of the pockets and pulls out a roll of cash. She finds an opened envelope with a name on it – it says 'Gus Delario'. Linda realises who it is. She takes the money.*

Cut.

INT. HOTEL ROOM. DAY.

Gus is going through his wallet, looking through books, and in pockets.

GUS

God, I thought I had more cash. I'll be right back.

LINDA
(*out of shot*)

It's OK, Bill.

GUS

There's an ATM downstairs right? I saw it in the –

LINDA
(*out of shot*)

You can only get three hundred out. There's a limit.

GUS

You're kidding.

LINDA
(*out of shot*)

No.

GUS

I feel terrible.

Linda opens the door.

LINDA

You should. You should feel really terrible and ashamed.

GUS

Ann.

LINDA

Excuse me.

Linda leaves the room, leaves Gus standing in his robe.

Cut.

EXT. CAFÉ. DAY.

Nicholas and Catherine are having coffee.

NICHOLAS

That's because it's not about having a beginning, a middle, and an end. It's an ongoing conversation that's taking place outside the venues where discourse is controlled and censored, like the mainstream media. It's keeping people in touch with what's going on.

CATHERINE

Uh-huh.

NICHOLAS

So how do you judge someone? An artist's work, I mean. I'm asking you.

CATHERINE

Batting average. If an actor's made twenty films and eight of them are actually worth seeing more than once, that's a forty per cent average. Hall of Fame time.

NICHOLAS

Eight of twenty worth remembering? You're living in a fantasy.

CATHERINE

It's not a long list, that's for sure. You might be on it some day.

NICHOLAS

That's a nice thing to say.

CATHERINE

It's business. I can't write about someone I don't believe in.

NICHOLAS

So you only write success stories?

Cut.

EXT. FILM SET. DAY.

Calvin and Francesca, between takes.

Beat.

CALVIN

How could she not?

FRANCESCA

Because the way it's written, she is out of his league.

CALVIN

But what about the letter?

FRANCESCA

I think the letter is stupid. I don't think people are going to get the letter.

Beat.

CALVIN

You have cat breath.

Cut.

INT. LEE'S OFFICE. DAY.

Lee is grilling another woman, who is currently stepping down off a chair. She hands Lee the beach ball.

LEE

Just a few more questions.

She motions for her to sit down again.

ROBERTA

I'd rather stand.

LEE

This requires that you sit.

ROBERTA

I can think better on my feet.

LEE

I don't doubt that for one second, Roberta, but trust me. You'll get tired if you stand for this portion of the review.

Roberta sits down and is in obvious discomfort. Lee deflates the beach ball and begins squeezing the air out of it.

LEE

There. Are you comfortable?

ROBERTA

I'm fine.

Lee pulls a pair of handcuffs out of her purse. She walks slowly to Roberta's chair.

LEE

Good. Relax.

She handcuffs her to the chair. They lock eyes.

LEE

Do you want tea or anything? Coffee? You're probably a coffee drinker. Right?

ROBERTA

Nothing for me, thanks.

LEE

They say it's Bloody Friday, Roberta. I'm sure you've noticed.

ROBERTA

Yes.

LEE

We have to cut some corners.

ROBERTA

I understand.

LEE

Today a man, tomorrow a mouse.

ROBERTA

That's a bit cruel, don't you think?

LEE

It's just an expression. Do you find me attractive?

ROBERTA

What? Um. Yes.

LEE

In what sort of way?

ROBERTA

In a human sort of way.

LEE

What parts of me do you find particularly attractive?

ROBERTA

You stand well.

LEE

Ah.

ROBERTA

Your hair has a silky texture. I would imagine.

LEE

Go on.

ROBERTA

And your hips are very stable.

Lee closes her eyes.

LEE

What colour are my eyes?

ROBERTA

I can't tell.

Lee opens them and looks at Roberta.

LEE

It's been a confusing day.

Cut.

INT. THEATRE. DAY.

Calvin is talking to the actor that plays 'Ed', Arty. They are watching a rehearsal of the Hitler black-out sketches. Currently the actor playing Hitler is getting hip-hop dance instruction from a choreographer.

CALVIN

Arty. The Internet?

ARTY

Yeah. We're supposed to meet in Tucson tomorrow. She thinks I'm a twenty-two-year-old painter. The art I can fake, but how do I wipe two decades off my face?

CALVIN

What happened to whatshername?

ARTY

Which?

CALVIN

From the grill at Universal. She was sexy.

ARTY

Oh. Yeah. I found her in the bathroom with a red rubber ball in her mouth.

CALVIN

What?

ARTY

I was staying over at her house, and I notice that she's gotten up in the middle of the night, and I see the bathroom light is on, and I push open the door and she's standing in front of the mirror with a red rubber ball in her mouth. Looking at herself. And she turns to me, takes the red rubber ball out of her mouth, and says, 'Do you need to go?'

CALVIN

Bullshit.

ARTY

Ask her out. Actually, you can't ask her out, she's a racist. I was willing to overlook that until the ball thing. Anyway.

They both look over at Hitler, who is trying out various hip-hop moves.

CALVIN

So what's the appeal of the Internet woman?

ARTY

She reminds me of – I don't know. There was this girl scout in my neighbourhood growing up.

CALVIN

Oh yeah?

ARTY

Donna Mason. God.

CALVIN

And?

ARTY

And everything. She was so good.

CALVIN

And?

ARTY

I was so – well, I had these visions.

CALVIN

I'm sure you did.

ARTY

I wanted to protect her. I could see dark things around her.

CALVIN

Donna?

ARTY

She had these strange eyes. Like, her pupils were down at the bottom instead of in the middle.

CALVIN

That's weird shit.

ARTY

Whenever I'd say, 'Hi Donna,' she'd turn around startled and look at me like this.

Arty tilts his head back and stares at Calvin.

CALVIN

Whoa –

ARTY

I know.

CALVIN

You do her?

ARTY

What?

CALVIN

What are you getting at, then?

ARTY

Did I *do* her? I just said I wanted to protect her.

CALVIN

All right, Superman – calm down. I was just wondering where you were headed with the girl scout story.

ARTY

Did I *do* her?

CALVIN

Sorry.

ARTY

Jesus, what's wrong with you?

CALVIN

I'm bored. Finish your story.

ARTY

There is no story. Donna had so many badges on her sash that she got bumped up to the next level.

CALVIN

Were you a boy scout?

ARTY

No.

CALVIN

The next level? I don't think there is a next level after girl scout.

ARTY

How do you know?

CALVIN

I was a boy scout.

ARTY

You?

CALVIN

Yes, sir. Scout's honour, sir.

ARTY

The next level is the same as boy scout – an eagle something.

CALVIN

Scout.

ARTY

Eagle scout. (*Beat, exhales.*) This is a disaster.

Beat.

I'm going to confess everything. As soon as I see her, I'm going to tell her the whole story. Enough lying. I'm not going to start it that way.

CALVIN

You're really gonna tell her?

ARTY

No.

Cut.

INT. HOTEL BAR. NIGHT.

Nicholas and his agent sit, nursing drinks. Catherine is with them, silent. The agent is looking at her most of the time.

NICHOLAS

Look, you liked it when you heard it, and you've told me when you haven't liked things. You *liked* it. So don't tell me you aren't going to pursue any more meetings on it, because this is what I want to do, seriously.

Beat.

Plus, it's gotten a lot better since you heard it. Ed and I have really beefed it up, worked out every scene. And I agree, I won't even bring up the stuff about me being in it. And even if they bring it up, we won't build it in. It actually is better if I don't, in the long run. If I want to establish my identity as a writer instead of an actor. Pinter started as an actor. Still acts, occasionally.

Beat.

NICHOLAS

This shit is cyclical, you know that.

Beat. Nicholas indicates the check.

I got it.

Cut.

EXT. CARL AND LEE'S HOUSE. DAY.

Carl drives up to his house. He gets out of his car and sees his across-the-street neighbour unloading groceries still dressed as a vampire. They exchange a wave.

Cut.

INT. CARL AND LEE'S KITCHEN. DAY.

Carl goes through the mail, listens to messages.

LEE

(*voice-over*)

Carl, you there? Pick up. Look, just put the brownies in that tin under the sink. It's more understated, and don't tie a ribbon around it or anything. And don't eat any. All right? And don't be late. And don't –

He crosses to the refrigerator and takes out a beer. Instinctively, he grabs a glass, opens the beer, and begins to pour. He then stops and begins considering this activity. He takes a sip of beer from the bottle, thinks for a moment, then continues pouring the beer into the glass.

Carl then turns the answering machine off.

He goes over to the brownie tray where he left it on top of the stove – only to find it on the floor with a large section eaten out of the middle.

CARL

Django!!!

Cut.

INT. LEE'S CAR. DAY.

Lee is stuck in traffic – a gridlock. She strains to see the cause of it. Three large movie trucks are blocking the lanes ahead. She lets out a long operatic note.

LEE

Fucking movies. Fucking overpaid fucking unhappy childhood fuckers. Fucking movie fucking fuckers.

She pulls out of traffic and into a parking spot.

Cut.

INT. HOTEL LOBBY. DAY.

Linda walks through the lobby with her table. She passes the concierge.

LINDA

'Night, Danny.

DANNY

Oh. Linda.

LINDA

Yeah?

DANNY

The gentleman in 205 left this for you.

Danny hands Linda a gift bag with an envelope sticking out of it.

Cut.

EXT. FILM SET. DAY.

Calvin and Francesca are talking.

CALVIN

I'm going to try something.

FRANCESCA

Oh God, Calvin, what?

CALVIN

I'm going to try something after you say, 'It never turns out like that.'

FRANCESCA

Why?

CALVIN

Just – I'm just going to try something.

FRANCESCA

Like what?

Calvin makes a call on his cell phone. He waits for an answer.

CALVIN

Just ride with it.

FRANCESCA

After 'It never turns out like that'?

CALVIN

Yeah.

Calvin walks away for privacy on his cell phone. Francesca practises her lines.

CALVIN

Lucy. Hey. Something has come up. I just found out I have this dinner. Yeah, oh – right, Carl. You do? Well, I didn't just find out – It's for our producer, Gus. He's forty and we're all – well – it's – no, it's not that – it's – yeah – yeah – uh – of course I do – God. Right. You are – no, no, you are. Can you meet me at the hotel? Uh, seven-thirty in the lobby.

Cut.

INT. LEE'S CLOSET. NIGHT.

Carl is on the phone, pacing. Django, Carl and Lee's dog, is passed out on a row of Lee's shoes. Carl leans down to touch Django and look for sighs of life.

Cut.

INT. THEATRE STAGE. DAY.

Hitler lies on a couch, watched over by an actor playing Freud. Arty, slouching in the fourth row, watches through his fingers.

HITLER

I'm just so tired of telling my story.

Beat.

You meet someone, and you think, Oh, I've got to tell them everything, just like I told the one before and the one before that . . . where I went to school, what did my father do, blah blah blah.

Beat.

It's boring. I'm bored with myself.

Freud nods, understanding. Then he glances at his watch.

FREUD

I'm sorry, but we're out of –

Hitler turns to him and stares.

FREUD

Please continue.

Cut.

INT. SEX SHOP. NIGHT.

Lee is looking at a row of sex toys. Her cell phone rings deep within her bag. She answers.

LEE

Yeah?

LINDA

(*voice-over*)

I can't

LEE

Why?

LINDA
(*voice-over*)

I just –

LEE

You just want to stay at home and watch your neighbours fuck?

LINDA
(*voice-over*)

Yeah. I –

LEE

Are you crying?

LINDA
(*voice-over*)

I kind of met your friend Gus.

LEE

Now there's a guy who can change your life.

Beat.

LINDA
(*voice-over*)

I have to go.

LEE

See you in the hotel lobby, seven-thirty.

She hangs up, her phone rings again. She looks to see who it is, sees it's Carl, rolls her eyes and drops it back into her bag ringing, until it stops.

Cut.

INT. LEE'S CLOSET. NIGHT.

Carl paces with the phone. Hangs up – dials another number. It rings for a while.

CARL

Come on, please. – Yeah, uh, listen, I read somewhere that chocolate can kill dogs and my dog uh – yeah, he's uh –

about twelve brownies – about twelve, ha – um, could you just send someone? – You don't? – Induce – Uh, OK. I could try.

Carl leans down and opens Django's eyes. They are rolled back in his head.

CARL

He might be dreaming. I, uh – OK.

Carl rolls up his sleeves.

Cut.

INT. SEX SHOP. NIGHT.

Two men at the cash register talk in low voices and look at Lee.

Cut.

INT. LEE'S CLOSET. NIGHT.

Carl is sweating, holding Django, who is now on all fours vomiting all over Lee's shoes. Carl holds the phone on his shoulder.

CARL

Oh God. – How long? Come on, Django – get it out – just let it out, baby – just – what? Yeah, but I need to move him now. We're in my wife's – what? OK. That's a good boy. That's it. Good boy. God. He's going to get dehydrated. OK – yeah. He's stopping. Yeah? – One, two, three, four – OK – yeah. OK. Right. Thanks. I will. Right.

Carl picks Django up like a baby and carries him down to the kitchen, cooing to him for comfort.

Cut.

INT. KITCHEN. NIGHT.

Carl fills a huge bowl of water for Django, who starts to doze again.

CARL

Come on. Wake up, dude. Drink, Django, drink it down.

Carl puts some water in his hand. Django drinks from that.

CARL

Yeah. It's water, D –it's magic water. It will change you. It will save you. It will make all your wishes come true.

Carl starts to cry from relief. He scoops another scoop of water and Django drinks from his hands.

Cut.

INT. DRESS SHOP. NIGHT.

Linda is paying for an outfit. She is paying cash.

CASHIER

It really looks great on you.

Linda does not say a word. She smiles at the cashier and leaves quickly.

Cut.

INT. SEX SHOP. NIGHT.

Lee is purchasing something. It has already been put in a thin plastic bag.

LEE

Can you wrap that please?

MAN I

No.

LEE

No?

MAN 2

Yeah. No.

LEE

Oh. OK. Well, thank you. Did you give me my credit card back?

MAN I

Yeah. Come back soon.

Lee goes through her purse to look for the credit card. She is holding her purse below the counter.

LEE
(*pissed*)
All right, you know what, that's it –

She goes for something (or appears to go for something) in her purse and the guys think it's a weapon. Man 2 suddenly slams her against the wall and twists her arm behind her back.

MAN 2
Drop it. Drop the fucking purse.

Man 1 points a gun at her.

Lee's face is pure terror.

Cut.

INT. KITCHEN. NIGHT.

Carl makes another call, looks through a list of phone numbers.

Cut.

INT. SEX SHOP. NIGHT.

Lee's cell phone rings from her bag on the floor. She cries while the men mumble to each other.

Cut.

INT. KITCHEN. NIGHT.

Carl finds the number he's looking for and hangs up from calling Lee. He calls Dr Green, his vet. While he's waiting for an answer, he sees a letter addressed to him personally. He seems to recognise it as Lee's handwriting, but as he is reaching for it his attention is diverted by a voice on the line:

CARL
Yes, hi, this is Carl Bright. Is this Dr Green's answering service? – Oh. Hi. Well, this is Carl Bright of – you do? – right. That was you? Yeah, Django loved it – loved you.

Heather. Right. – Yeah, he is – he's a sweet – right. Listen, Heather, Django is in trouble. He got into some chocolate – I know – some brownies. I've already done that – yeah – I just wonder if Dr Green could come have a quick look at him – He is? – Oh. – Right. – Yeah? I just want to make sure he's not going to die, you know? – I know – well, great, you could? So – OK – right – thank you – oh, the address. Right. You would need the address.

Cut.

INT. SEX SHOP. NIGHT.

Lee is still standing against the wall. She is crying. Man 1 and Man 2 are trying to console her.

MAN 1

We weren't sure. But when you reached into your bag like that – we –

MAN 2

We thought it was her.

MAN 1

We were expecting things to get ugly. You know? We'd been warned about her. She's like . . . insane.

MAN 2

And you look just like her. It's weird.

MAN 1

Well, her hair's a little different.

Lee has turned around and is leaning on the wall, looking at them in disbelief.

Cut.

INT. LINDA'S APT. NIGHT.

Linda has transformed herself. She is putting on the finishing touches. She sees her neighbours having sex across the street.

Then:

EXT. LINDA'S APT. NIGHT.

Linda gets into her car. She looks across the street. The street is empty except for an old woman walking her dog, who notices Linda and smiles. Linda gets into her car and admires herself in the rear-view mirror.

Cut.

INT. HOTEL BAR. NIGHT.

Nicholas, his agent, and Catherine stand up to leave their table.

AGENT

I have to admire you for your belief in this project. But the reality is another thing altogether. It's all market-place shit and I don't think this is a good role for you. So don't even push that. When does this article come out?

CATHERINE

In a couple of months.

AGENT

Call if you can't get any answers out of this guy.

He hands Catherine his card and winks.

CATHERINE

Thanks. Great to meet you.

AGENT

Nice seeing you.

He winks again, shakes Nicholas's hand, and leaves.

NICHOLAS

Smug bastard.

Nicholas passes out. Catherine catches him.

Cut.

INT. KITCHEN. NIGHT.

Carl opens the door and sees Heather, mid-thirties, the after-hours vet for Dr Green.

CARL

Heather.

HEATHER

Carl.

CARL

Thank you for coming.

HEATHER

Where is he?

Heather sees Django by his water bowl. She breaks out into doggy sing-song voice.

HEATHER

Oh. Django boy – there's a little biscuit, boy. Hello. Hello, furry friend. Hello.

She buries her face in his fur. He wags his tail. She looks up and sees the tray still filled with crumbs in the sink. She also sees a used piece of aluminium foil on the counter.

HEATHER

Did Mommy and Daddy feed you bad brownies? Bad bad bad brownies? Bad bad Mommy and Daddy.

Django wags his tail. Heather stands up and faces Carl.

CARL

God, he loves you. He's usually so –

HEATHER

What else was in the brownies besides chocolate?

CARL

You mean, ingredients?

HEATHER

Yeah, like hash?

CARL

Something my wife brought back from London. We made them for a friend. He's forty today and we –

Heather smells the jar. She softens.

HEATHER

It's so much better than pot. Right?

CARL

Uh.

HEATHER

I haven't smoked it in years, though. God, when I was in my twenties, I channelled Joni Mitchell on hash. My neighbour was this guitar player and I would just make up lyrics while he played. Our songs would end up with all these odd rhyme schemes and –

CARL

Is he going to be all right?

Cut.

INT. LIMO. NIGHT.

Calvin and Francesca are talking.

CALVIN

Because he's balleemic.

FRANCESCA

Bulimic.

CALVIN

He throws up his food. It's never real.

FRANCESCA

Do you think that's believable?

CALVIN

I've never seen that done before, have you?

FRANCESCA

It is kind of unusual for a man to –

CALVIN

And I think he has body issues.

FRANCESCA

You do?

Cut.

INT. HOTEL LOBBY. NIGHT.

Lee is waiting in the lobby. She is seated, watching people pass. She makes a call on her cell phone.

Cut.

INT. KITCHEN. NIGHT.

The brownie dish is empty.

Carl and Heather sit on the floor on either side of Django. They are both stroking Django and cooing to him – obviously stoned. The phone rings and Carl looks at it – does not answer it. The answering machine goes on but the caller hangs up.

Cut.

INT. HOTEL LOBBY. NIGHT.

Calvin and Francesca arrive. Calvin sees Lee and drops Francesca's arm. Lee does not see Calvin.

FRANCESCA

You know her?

CALVIN

No.

FRANCESCA

Carl's wife.

CALVIN

Yeah?

FRANCESCA

I've heard things.

CALVIN

Yeah. Yeah?

Calvin sees Lucy, kisses her, meeting Lee's stare.

CALVIN

Franny, this is –

LUCY

Franny, it's Lucy Morgan from *LA Magazine*.

FRANCESCA

I'm sorry I –

LUCY

The Sedona piece?

FRANCESCA

Oh. Oh God. *Hey*. How *are* you? Your hair's different. God.

LUCY

Great. I work with Carl.

FRANCESCA

And you know Cal from –

CALVIN

Where's this dinner?

Linda walks into the lobby looking gorgeous and carrying the gift bag that she has gotten from the concierge. We follow her over to Lee.

LINDA

So where's this party?

Lee looks at Linda as if she sees a ghost.

LEE

God.

LINDA

What?

She can't speak. Linda sits beside her.

Cut.

INT. HOTEL LOBBY. NIGHT.

Calvin and Lucy and Francesca are still talking. A man with a normal face approaches Francesca.

SAM

Franny Davis?

FRANCESCA

Yes?

SAM

Sam Osborne.

Francesca blanks.

FRANCESCA

I'm sorry – I –

SAM

The Duchess of Malfi – Berkshires – lighting guy.

FRANCESCA

Sam Osborne. *Hey*. Oh my God. Are you here for –

SAM

Gus's fortieth. Yeah. 'I feel like a waitress on vacation.' Remember that?

FRANCESCA

Yeah. God. Well, I was. God, you remember that?

SAM

Yeah, I do.

FRANCESCA

God.

They look at each other for a moment.

SAM

Listen, I don't want to bug you, I just wanted to say how happy I am for you. I always thought you had something special, and it's great what you've been able to do.

FRANCESCA

Well, shit, Sam, don't just say something like that and run off on me. Walk me to the party.

Cut.

INT. PRIVATE DINING ROOM. NIGHT.

The room is full of people sitting at different tables. Everyone seems to be waiting for Gus, who has not arrived. Lee and Linda walk by Calvin's table. She catches his eye.

LEE

Hello. You must be Calvin Cummings.

CALVIN

Yes. Your husband has written a beautiful script.

They stare at each other for a time. Lucy breaks the tension.

LUCY

Lee, Lucy Morgan. – *LA Magazine*. I work with Carl. Or at least I did until today.

LEE

Well, I'm sorry.

LUCY

Oh. No, I'm sorry.

Cut.

INT. LIVING ROOM. NIGHT.

Carl and Heather are sitting in large comfortable chairs. Django is lying on the rug between them.

HEATHER

Lolita Honeysuckle.

Carl and Heather laugh. The phone rings.

Cut.

EXT. PRIVATE DINING ROOM. NIGHT.

Lee is calling Carl on her cell phone, drinking a cocktail. She paces.

Later:

INT. PRIVATE DINING ROOM. NIGHT.

Still no Gus. Calvin is making a little speech about Gus's legendary tardiness to keep people entertained.

CALVIN

I could tell you another Gus Being Late story, but my favourite moment was when Gus called at one-twenty in the morning to ask me what I really thought of him.

PARTYGOER

What did you say?

CALVIN

I said, 'Gus, whatever I think of you isn't going to change before ten o'clock in the morning.' And I hung up.

Lee sits back at her table. Lucy looks up at Calvin in total admiration.

LEE

Blow this up. I'm too drunk.

LINDA

What is that?

LEE

It's a beach ball. It inflates quickly. Hurry.

Linda blows up the beach ball. No one notices her. People laugh at what Calvin says.

CALVIN

And I'm sure some of you can top that.

The actor who plays the agent stands up from his table where he's sitting with the actors that play the studio executives.

ACTOR/AGENT

Gus and I used to hunt together. We were waiting up in this deer stand and Gus climbed down to relieve himself in the bushes. I heard him but I couldn't see him. And then I couldn't hear him any more. I waited to hear a rustle or even a scream – but nothing. Finally, it got dark and I went on back to the cabin. Well sir, there was Gus, just sitting pretty as you please by the fire. I say, 'Gus, what's up?' and he says, 'I was cold.'

People are not responding so well to this story.

Cut.

INT. HOTEL BAR. NIGHT.

Catherine is reviving Nicholas, touching him, force-feeding him water. He wakes up, realises where he is.

NICHOLAS

Did I –?

CATHERINE

Yeah you –

NICHOLAS

I am – God – I'm so sorry.

CATHERINE

Are you all right?

NICHOLAS

Yeah. This – I have to ask you something.

CATHERINE

What?

NICHOLAS

I need for you to come back to New York with me.

CATHERINE

I can't. I –

NICHOLAS

It's the letter. I can't stop thinking about the letter.

CATHERINE

That was –

NICHOLAS

It was beautiful. We belong together.

CATHERINE

That doesn't make sense.

NICHOLAS

No one has ever written a love letter to me before.

CATHERINE

But I –

NICHOLAS

You were there. You are here. Think about it. We can work more on the story – take it from there.

CATHERINE

But it never works out like that – it –

Catherine continues to wipe his forehead, comfort him. He kisses her passionately.

Even the real Calvin and Francesca are shocked.

Cut.

INT. PRIVATE DINING ROOM. NIGHT.

Lee throws the beach ball at Calvin and hits him. He picks it up, laughs and throws it back to her. Everyone turns to look at Lee. She fires it back at him with a question.

LEE

Name all the countries in Africa, Calvin.

A murmur goes through the crowd. He does not throw the ball back.

CALVIN

I think Gus would understand if we started our meals. Let's eat.

People applaud. Calvin walks back to his table. He throws the ball at Lee. Lee comes over to him.

CALVIN

What do you want from me?

LEE

Some closure, Cal. Does your new girlfriend know that you fucked the screenwriter's wife this afternoon just before you dumped her?

CALVIN

Uh –

LUCY

Yes, Lee. He told me. Now why don't you go back to your table and sober up?

Linda comes over and takes Lee back to the table. Lee is stunned.

LINDA

I have to take care of something. Just sit here and don't move. Carl will be here soon.

Lee just stares straight ahead.

INT. HOTEL. NIGHT.

Linda is walking towards Gus's room with the gift bag. She puts the bag down and turns to see a chambermaid that knows her. She is startled.

CHAMBERMAID

Oh, miss. You are beautiful.

LINDA

Thanks, Irene.

IRENE

You are working?

LINDA

No. I left something in here. Can you let me in for a second?

IRENE

Of course.

Irene lets her in and winks at her. She walks down the hall. Linda closes the door.

Cut.

INT. HOTEL ROOM. NIGHT.

Linda walks to the bathroom and puts the gift bag, which has the torn envelope with the wad of cash in it, on the counter. In the mirror we see Gus, apparently asleep, on his bed. Linda does not see him. She decides to pee. As she sits down she sees him, and a look of horror comes over her face. She slams the door.

Cut.

INT. PRIVATE DINING ROOM. NIGHT.

Lee is standing in her chair, holding the beach ball in her arms. She is very drunk.

LEE

. . . all steamed up and he just knocked on my window and said, in his unique, charming Gus fashion, 'Have you been waiting long?' I thought he was making fun of me. I mean I was wearing a linen suit, for God's sake, and I had mascara all over my face. I was the only car in the parking lot and I – (*She laughs.*)

People stare at her. Her cell phone rings.

LEE

Carl? . . . Oh.

Beat.

Where are you? He's *what*?

Cut.

INT. CARL AND LEE'S HOUSE. NIGHT.

Carl and Heather, each staring off into space.

CARL

See, there are three types of movement in any arc of motion. Acceleration, when you are going faster than you were before; Stasis, the one instant in which you are neither going faster than before nor slower than before, the absolute mid-point of the event; and Deceleration, where you are going slower than you were, until finally you stop.

HEATHER

I may have to call a taxi to get home.

Cut.

INT. HOTEL ROOM. NIGHT.

Lee is standing next to Linda by Gus's bed. They stare at Gus's obviously dead body, which lies on the bed with a towel around its waist. Linda is holding the gift bag we saw her earlier placing in the bathroom – the gift bag with the wad of cash.

LINDA

We should tell somebody, right?

LEE

Who?

LINDA

The hotel. I'll say I forgot something in his room and he didn't answer, and –

LEE

And?

A beat as Linda thinks how this will sound.

LINDA

Right.

Another beat.

LINDA

This is just . . . a few hours ago he was alive. Really alive.

Beat.

Do you think I left fingerprints?

LEE

What? No. You were in here before, right, to give him a massage?

LINDA

Yeah. Did you touch the door handle on the way in?

LEE

No. I don't think so. No.

Lee sits down and lights a cigarette.

LINDA

I know what I'm supposed to say in a situation like this, but I don't feel like saying it. Can you smoke in these rooms?

Lee ignores her. Linda goes over to look at Gus. She peeks under the towel.

LEE

Have you ever known a man who looked perfectly desirable at a distance but morphed into a freak at close range?

Beat.

LINDA

It's so easy to forgive someone when they're dead.

Beat.

Why did you marry Carl?

Lee looks at Linda to judge why she's been asked this question, but Linda's back is to her. She decides to take the question seriously.

LEE

He keeps trying, even when he knows the situation is hopeless.

Linda peruses Gus's suitcase.

LINDA

He brought his own flashlight.

LEE

Why? Linda.

LINDA

I just thought of it.

LEE

What made you think of it?

LINDA

I don't know. Was Gus a smoker?

Cut.

INT. PRIVATE DINING ROOM. NIGHT.

People eat and talk. They've stopped thinking about Gus.

Lucy, Calvin, Sam and Francesca are sitting at the same table. They all eat enthusiastically and play a game.

LUCY

OK, we go around and everyone says the first thing that comes to their mind. Anyone can change categories as long as it's food related. But the first person to complete five rounds without hesitating gets to change to another subject. OK, I'll start. What about comfort food?

CALVIN

Mashed potatoes.

SAM

Caramel corn.

FRANCESCA

Caramel corn?

LUCY

No judgements.

FRANCESCA

Corn on the cob.

LUCY

Cream of wheat.

CALVIN

Peanut butter.

SAM

Chocolate.

FRANCESCA

OK, what about food you'd eat out of desperation?

They eat quietly and consider this.

Cut.

INT. THEATRE STAGE. NIGHT.

Hitler, lying on a couch, speaking to Freud. There is a very small audience in attendance.

HITLER

All the world loves a Winner. Isn't that what people think? Why do they love the Winner? Because they think he knows something. He had to know something, in order to win. So we admire him. But the Winner doesn't learn anything from winning. No. The Loser learns something. About himself. Losing teaches you about yourself. So the Loser is the Winner. Not in actual terms of course – I'm speaking figuratively.

Hitler looks around at Freud. Freud smiles and nods.

HITLER

(*beat*)

I have something else to go into, but not if I can't finish it. How much time do we have?

Some in the audience exchange glances.

Cut.

INT. BACKSTAGE. NIGHT.

The actor who played Hitler is talking to Arty.

ACTOR

I appreciate that, really. Coming from someone who writes *and* acts, well . . . thank you for saying that. I feel like it's come after me now. For a while I was going after it, but now it's come after me. It's good.

ARTY

Great.

ACTOR

Yeah.

Beat.

ACTOR

It's writers like you and Carl, really. Where is Carl?

ARTY

He had to go to a party.

ACTOR

Right. That producer guy's fortieth. Not shabby.

ARTY

Gus. Delario.

ACTOR

Carl owns the tuxedo, eh?

ARTY

Yeah.

Beat.

I told you about tomorrow, right?

ACTOR

Yeah. Hey, good luck. Be bold.

ARTY

Thanks.

ACTOR

'Ann.' It's a nice name. It's gonna go good.

Cut.

INT. KITCHEN. NIGHT.

Lee comes home late and rather drunk. She hears voices in the living room. She listens.

CARL

(*out of shot*)

You see, my wife and I were having some trouble. I . . . suggested that perhaps we were in a rut and we should try something new. And she said, 'Like what?' And I said, 'Well, like why don't we tape ourselves doing it?' And she was just shocked by that, thought it was beyond disgusting.

Few months go by, then she says one night, out of the blue: 'OK, I'll do it.'

HEATHER

Whoa.

CARL

So then we get all set up to do it, I get it all ready, and she's ready, and she's gone out and gotten herself a little . . . *toy* to use in the video. Actually, it wasn't a little toy, it was quite a big toy. In fact, it was too big a toy. When I saw it – I knew I wouldn't be able to . . . I couldn't. We haven't. And there's just no going back from that. Either she lost respect for me, or I lost respect for me, or something. Something was lost.

HEATHER

Yeah. So what will you do?

CARL

I have no idea. I've decided what I'm going to do professionally. I want to teach again.

Beat.

I don't feel like I've learned a single thing in my life, and yet I loved teaching. That's the legacy of higher education.

HEATHER

But what about your wife?

CARL

I'll hope we get over it.

Beat.

I don't know. In addition to loving her, I just really like her. But I think she feels everything and everyone is against her, somehow. It keeps her from being happy.

Lee is crying. We follow her to the living room. She sits down with Heather and Carl.

HEATHER

Oh God.

CARL

Hi.

LEE

Hi.

CARL

Oh. Lee, this is Heather, Dr Green's assistant.

Lee is petting Django, who is sound asleep.

LEE

Hello.

CARL

Django ate the brownies. Are you all right?

LEE

Gus had a heart attack during his afternoon nap. He's dead.

Carl tries to clear his head enough to grasp this. Lee continues petting Django and crying.

HEATHER

I should –

CARL

Yeah. Thanks, Heather. Thanks for stopping by.

HEATHER

(*to Lee*)

It was nice to meet you.

Carl walks Heather out.

Lee continues to cry and pet Django. Carl comes back and sits with Lee. They are quiet for a while.

She looks at him.

LEE

Carl, for two years, I've been having an –

CARL

I know, Lee. I know.

A long beat.

When I was five I knew the name of every form of currency in the world. It's been downhill ever since.

Another beat.

LEE

I just want this day to be over.

Cut.

EXT. LINDA'S APT. NIGHT.

Linda drives into her driveway. She gets out of her car. Her neighbour is leaning against a car in front of his house, making out with a different woman than we've seen before.

LINDA

(*shouting*)

Can you name all the countries in Africa?

The couple part and stare at her.

Cut.

INT. PRIVATE DINING ROOM. NIGHT.

Francesca and Sam are the only ones left in the private dining room. They are involved in an intense discussion. The cleaning crew cleans up around them.

Cut.

INT. CAR. DAY.

Nicholas rides to the airport alone.

Cut.

INT. AIRPORT. DAY.

Nicholas is waiting at the airport alone. He opens his briefcase and finds another letter with his name on it. He looks around. He opens the letter. Reads the first line. 'Nicholas, I will begin simply: I love you.' He looks around. He continues reading. 'Have always loved you.' Catherine approaches and sits down with some amount of purpose.

Nicholas looks at her, thinking a moment before he says:

NICHOLAS

Catherine.

CATHERINE

Nicholas.

THESE WORDS SCROLL ACROSS THE BOTTOM OF THE SCREEN:

SEARCHING FOR SATELLITE SIGNAL
PLEASE STAND BY

Cut.

INT. AIRPORT. DAY.

Linda is reading Los Angeles Magazine *at the gate. Arty is sitting across from her, reading* The Art Book. *He is staring at her. She looks at him and smiles, then back to her magazine. There is a muffled announcement made. She listens for a minute. Then back to her magazine.*

LINDA

Did you get that?

ARTY

No.

LINDA

Are you on the flight to Tucson?

ARTY

Yeah.

LINDA

So this must be the right gate.

ARTY

Are you Russian?

LINDA

No.

ARTY

You're supposed to say, 'Am I russian where?'

They laugh.

Cut.

INT. CARL AND LEE'S HOUSE. MORNING.

Carl is reading the New York Times *at the kitchen table. Lee enters in her bathrobe, sleepy.*

LEE

You got *LA*?

CARL

Happy birthday.

He hands her an unwrapped LA Times *from a nearby chair.*

LEE

Thank you. Have any interesting dreams last night?

CARL

No. The usual. I had an afro this time.

She takes the paper and begins to shuffle off. She stops upon seeing the handwritten letter addressed to Carl. Without being spotted by Carl, she takes the still-unopened envelope and leaves the kitchen. In the hallway, she tears it up and throws it into a waste basket.

Cut.

INT. PLANE. DAY.

Nicholas and Catherine look at each other as the plane takes off. They kiss.

Insert:

Fireworks, explosions, birds taking flight, etc.

A title card is superimposed. It reads:

THE END?

Cut.

INT. PLANE. DAY.

Linda and Arty are sitting near each other.

ARTY

Ever been to Tucson?

LINDA

No, not personally.

He smiles. She smiles back.

Cut.

INT. THEATRE STAGE. DAY.

The actor playing Hitler is getting dressed in front of a bureau with a mirror. On the bureau are a glass of water and a large black capsule.

HITLER

A moment of inspiration, that's all anybody wants. To have an original idea, to fall in love.

Beat.

It takes courage to surrender to these things. Especially if you have – (*makes air quotes*) – 'control issues'. I get that a lot.

Beat.

It's hard to stay present.

He takes the large pill, swallows it along with the glass of water.

HITLER

I know what people will talk about, when they talk about me. People are petty. They'll talk about the moustache. They'll say, 'What was up with the moustache? Didn't he know it was Chaplin's moustache?' Of course I knew. Chaplin had it first, but Chaplin didn't understand it.

He crosses to a bed and lies down. After a moment:

HITLER

This room smells like coconuts.

Cut.

INT. APARTMENT. DAWN.

Calvin is sitting on the edge of a bed, looking down at:

Lucy, naked on the unmade bed. An almost identical recreation of our opening frame, in fact.

Title card:

FULL FRONTAL
(*tentative*)

Insert computer screen, as we see this card typed out. The cursor moves to the print command and instructs the printer to print this text.

Carl rises from his chair in front of a computer and crosses to a printer. Out of the printer comes a single sheet of paper containing these words:

FULL FRONTAL
(*tentative*)
Begin End Titles

And we begin end titles.